FIGHTING TO WIN

Volume One
The Nature and Scope of Spiritual Warfare

Victorious Christian Life Series

Victorious Christian Life Series

FIGHTING TO WIN

Volume One
The Nature and Scope of Spiritual Warfare

By Onoyom E. Ekanem

Victorious Christian Life Series

Unless otherwise indicated, all scripture in this publication are taken from King James Version of the HOLY BIBLE or paraphrased by the author.

Scripture quotations marked (NIV) are taken from the HOLY BIBLE, NEW INTERNATIONAL VERSION®. NIV®. Copyright©1973, 1978, 1984 by International Bible Society. Used by permission of Zondervan. All rights reserved.

Scripture quotations marked (NLT) are taken from the Holy Bible, New Living Translation, copyright © 1996. Used by permission of Tyndale House Publishers, Inc., Wheaton, Illinois 60189. All rights reserved.

Scripture quotations marked "NKJV™" are taken from the New King James Version®. Copyright © 1982 by Thomas Nelson, Inc. Used by permission. All rights reserved.
AMP "Scripture quotations taken from the Amplified® Bible, Copyright © 1954, 1958, 1962, 1964, 1965, 1987 by The Lockman Foundation
Used by permission." (www.Lockman.org)

Fighting to Win Volume 1 – The Nature and Scope of Spiritual Warfare
Revised Printing
ISBN: 978-0-9786728-1-2
Copyright © 2013 by Onoyom E. Ekanem
376 Beach Farm Circle #367
Highland, MI 48357

Printed in the United States of America. All rights reserved under International copyright Law. Contents and /or cover may not be reproduced in whole or in part in any form without written permission from author and publisher.

Cover picture: Sunset over Pontiac Lake in White Lake Michigan by Lisa Ekanem

---

Victorious Christian Life Series

TABLE OF CONTENT

Foreword	i
Acknowledgement	iii
Dedication	iv
1) Introduction to Spiritual Warfare	1
2) Wake Up Oh Sleeping Giant	17
3) The Battle in Progress	49
4) The Arena of Spiritual Warfare	69
5) The Enemy of the Saints	89
6) The Organization of Your Enemy	109
7) The Weapons and Tricks of Your Enemy	125
8) Stand in the Evil Day	145

Victorious Christian Life Series

Victorious Christian Life Series

Foreword

Christians everywhere are encouraged through the word of God to, *"Fight the good fight of the faith."* This clearly points to the fact that Christians are not merely those who believe in God, and in the fundamental doctrine of salvation. We are soldiers of the cross who contend for the faith that was once delivered to the saints. We are heavenly bound creatures who should fight with every God given spiritual weapon, which by nature, is designed to defeat all unseen adversaries along the way.

These adversaries are among the many witnesses always present around us. Their mission is to deter us from God's purpose and will for our lives. With divers schemes they come to kill, to steal and to destroy, but we should not be ignorant of their activities and devices. Through Christ Jesus, God has given us all that we need to wage a spiritual warfare in which we are guaranteed victory.

Onoyom Ekanem authors *"Fighting to Win"* which is birthed out of many years of teaching and combat experience in spiritual warfare. He also draws from years of exercising spiritual authority from God, and teaching courses on the authority of the believer. This book offers believers at every level of maturity, a biblical based teaching on spiritual warfare.

This is Volume One of a two-volume book. In this volume, *"The Nature and Scope of Spiritual Warfare,"* you will get to know your enemy, his organization, targets, strategies, weapons and more. Volume Two, which follows shortly, concludes with a greater awareness of who and whose we are. It discusses the weapons that God has given us for spiritual warfare. In addition, it teaches us how we should use them to win our battles and sustain our victory. This book will be a blessing to you.

Bishop Charles H. Ellis III
Sr. Pastor, Greater Grace Temple
Presiding Bishop,
Pentecostal Assemblies of the World, Inc.

Acknowledgement

To my wonderful wife and partner Laury, thank you for your encouragement . Your unwavering prayer and intercession over the years and particularly while I was writing this book has been a treasure chest and a garrison of armor for our family.

Thanks also to my children Lisa, Angela, Bassey and Onoyom, for your sacrifice, support, and prayer as I wrote this book.

To my Pastor, Bishop Charles H. Ellis III, thank you for the allowing God to use you to bless the body of Christ. I appreciate your support and encouragement to me in the ministry to which God has called me. Thank you for the foreword and your support in promoting of this book as well as making it possible for me to teach courses in spiritual warfare. Greater Grace Temple, Detroit, Mi

To all my co-laborers at Greater Grace Temple, may God continue to bless the fruits of your labor. Thanks to the leadership team of the Christian Education Department and all my students over the years who have taken the courses on spiritual warfare.

Dedication

I dedicate this book to the GLORY and HONOR of my LORD and Savior JESUS CHRIST.

In addition, to the memory of all the pillars of the gospel, that God had placed in my life, and upon whose shoulders I stand. Prominent among them, my Father and Pastor, Chief Essien Bassey Ekanem, who raised me in a Christian household and taught me by example, how to be a good steward of Jesus Christ. My mother, Mrs. Edung Ekanem, Mother yours was a short and memorable visit, yet your legacy continues. To my brother, who was also my fellow soldier, and friend, Bassey Essien Ekanem.

I also dedicate this book to my Late Pastor, Bishop David Lee Ellis, Pastor, Greater Grace Temple, Detroit, Michigan, and Assistant Presiding Prelate of the Pentecostal Assemblies of the World, Inc. Who not only embraced me as one of his sheep, but also became my mentor and a father in the Gospel of Jesus Christ.

"14 But strong meat belongeth to them that are of full age, even those who by reason of use have their senses exercised to discern both good and evil."

(Hebrews 5:14)

"3 For though we walk in the flesh, we do not war after the flesh:"

(2nd Corinthians 10:3-6)

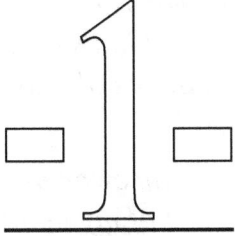

INTRODUCTION TO SPIRITUAL WARFARE

Spiritual warfare is an on going war of good versus evil and involves every living soul. I was careful not to say every Christian because it does not really matter whether you are Christian or not. If you are alive, you are a part of the warfare. You are either a part of the victorious army or a part of the losing army, either way; you are a part of it. For this warfare, some enlist, others are drafted and the rest are caught loitering aimlessly in the battlefield.

Yes, many today are wandering aimlessly through life. They know neither their source nor their destination. Consequently, and even more sadly, they do not know their purpose. They have simply become wandering souls, up for grabs, and subject to the rule of spiritual forces operating in the heavens. This is probably the most dangerous state we can find ourselves. For these people take neither the Almighty God nor the devil seriously. There is a saying that "if you cannot stand for something you will fall for anything." These simply go through life, falling for whatever it hands them, because of their failure to stand upon the promises of God. Therefore, the Bible declares:

"14 ...: These are the words of the Amen, the faithful and true witness, the ruler of God's creation. 15 I know your deeds, that you are neither cold nor hot. I wish you were either one or the other!

16 So, because you are lukewarm—neither hot nor cold—I am about to spit you out of my mouth.

17 You say, 'I am rich; I have acquired wealth and do not need a thing.' But you do not realize that you are wretched, pitiful, poor, blind and naked.

18 I counsel you to buy from me gold refined in the fire, so you can become rich; and white clothes to wear, so you can cover your shameful nakedness; and salve to put on your eyes, so you can see." Revelation 3:14-18 NIV

What an indictment. What a risk because of indecision. What a misplacement of life's foundation. What a waste of God's precious promises. We are vested with power and yet powerless, given to rule but living in subjection because for some reason, we have failed to hear the cry of David who admonishes as he cries saying:

"7 ¶ Lift up your heads, O ye gates; and be ye lift up, ye everlasting doors; and the King of glory shall come in.

8 Who is this King of glory? The LORD strong and mighty, the LORD mighty in battle.

9 Lift up your heads, O ye gates; even lift them up, ye everlasting doors; and the King of glory shall come in.

10 Who is this King of glory? The LORD of hosts, he is the King of glory. Selah." Psalms 24:7-10

When the King of glory comes, He comes to rebuild us and restore His rule in the void areas of our lives. He comes to give us grace and peace, from him which is, and which

Introduction to Spiritual Warfare

was, and which is to come; even our Lord Jesus Christ, who loved us so much that he washed us from our sins with his own blood, It is Him who said:

"19 Those whom I love I rebuke and discipline. So be earnest, and repent

20 Here I am! I stand at the door and knock. If anyone hears my voice and opens the door, I will come in and eat with him, and he with me.

21 To him who overcomes, I will give the right to sit with me on my throne, just as I overcame and sat down with my Father on his throne.

22 He who has an ear, let him hear what the Spirit says to the churches." Revelation 3:19-22 NIV

We are not exempt from the war because we refuse to be engaged in it. For one, we know that if we do not see it fit to acknowledge God in our life, He will eventually give up on us, for His Spirit will not pull on us forever. For He says:

"Now I will tell you what I am going to do to my vineyard: I will take away its hedge, and it will be destroyed; I will break down its wall, and it will be trampled."
Isaiah 5:5 NIV

The devil's technique is to seek out and draft the people that he finds in the idle state, perhaps because they are ignorant of their environment. That is why, people often say, that "the idle mind is the devil's workshop" for he knows that:

"He that diggeth a pit shall fall into it; and whoso breaketh an hedge, a serpent shall bite him."
Ecclesiastes 10:8

Therefore, these become possessed of the devil, which drives them to perform his wicked deeds and acts of disobedience. They made an entry by the devil possible, because they choose not to seek and abide under the shadow of the Almighty.

God on the other hand, can draft those who do acknowledge Him in their life, and who do keep themselves from being defiled by the world system, and yet not engaged in the battle in progress. He can also draw them and cause them to become unconsciously and systematically involved in this warfare before they come to a realization of what has been going on. Remember that Isaiah started prophesying in the beginning, but with the death of King Uzziah, he came to a greater realization of God and His desire for him. Therefore, we hear Isaiah saying

"6 Then said I, Woe is me! for I am undone; because I am a man of unclean lips, and I dwell in the midst of a people of unclean lips: for mine eyes have seen the King, the LORD of hosts . ...

8 Also I heard the voice of the Lord, saying, Whom shall I send, and who will go for us? Then said I, Here am I; send me." Isaiah 6:6, 8

Up until now, he had not said send me. When God says this is your time and your season, something will change in your life to draw your attention to the calling that is on you, and guide you as you walk toward that calling howbeit, with occasional struggle. This was the case with Abram, whom God called, and sent away from his father's house. Gideon, David, and Jeremiah are other examples of those that God drafted, and set in positions in his victorious army. Sometimes God can draft you and you do not even know it. To these people, God seems to say, "Before I formed you, I knew you and I ordained you. It does not really matter what

Introduction to Spiritual Warfare

your personal plans may be. I have a call on your life, and I'm going to cause things to happen in your life to lead you to what I had purposed for you." For these reluctant warriors, this is the stage when such questions as why me, or what did I do to deserve this, often come to mind. It is a time when you find yourself losing control of the events in your life as the Holy Ghost begins to order your steps. God drafted Moses, and because of this calling on him, he could not continue to enjoy the riches in Egypt. For it is said that.

> *"23 By faith Moses, when he was born, was hid three months of his parents, because they saw he was a proper child; and they were not afraid of the king's commandment.*
>
> *24 By faith Moses, when he was come to years, refused to be called the son of Pharaoh's daughter;*
>
> *25 Choosing rather to suffer affliction with the people of God, than to enjoy the pleasures of sin for a season;*
>
> *26 Esteeming the reproach of Christ greater riches than the treasures in Egypt: for he had respect unto the recompence of the reward.*
>
> *27 By faith he forsook Egypt, not fearing the wrath of the king: for he endured, as seeing him who is invisible."*
>
> *Hebrews 11:23-27*

Those who enlist are those who upon encounter with God, fall in love with Him and dedicate their lives to serving Him only. Being constrained by His love, they forsake all, and trust Him. As with Joshua, these have chosen God.

> *"And if it seem evil unto you to serve the LORD, choose you this day whom ye will serve; whether the gods which your fathers served that were on the other side of the*

> *flood, or the gods of the Amorites, in whose land ye dwell: but as for me and my house, we will serve the LORD."*
> *Joshua 24:15*

And, as with Timothy, they are committed to:

> *"Fight the good fight of faith, lay hold on eternal life, to which you were also called and have confessed the good confession in the presence of many witnesses."*
> *1st Timothy 6:12*

Those who enlisted are those who are sold out on Jesus. In spite of all their trials and struggles in life, they trust him and depend on Him as Simon Peter said, "Lord, to whom shall we go? thou hast the words of eternal life." They yearn for his presence and from the depth of their soul they cry:

> *"O God, thou art my God; early will I seek thee: my soul thirsteth for thee, my flesh longeth for thee in a dry and thirsty land, where no water is;" Psalms 63:1*

This battlefield is all-encompassing and is not in the natural realm even though its effect is felt in the natural. Whenever something happens in the spiritual realm, we feel the effect of it in the natural realm. Every time there is a "sneeze" in the spiritual realm, we catch a "cold" in the natural realm. That is why Jesus said your will be done on earth as it is in heaven. All things begin in the heavens and transition through to the natural realm. We do not need to get tangled in what we can see with our natural eyes, because the things that we can see are temporal, before we master them, they pass away. Before we can get a good description of our circumstance, it has already become history. Before we can figure out why things are happening to us the way they are happening, they are passed.

This warfare is not in the natural. It has nothing to do with you and me, but it has to do with God fighting the

Introduction to Spiritual Warfare

enemy of the saints and giving us charge as His ambassadors to be the ones responsible for enforcing His power, authority, control, and dominion on this side of heaven. You may think that when Satan raises his ugly head and begins to wreak havoc in your life that he is really after you. He does not care that much about you as a person. It is not you that he really cares about because you see, when God took Elijah into the heavens in the chariot of fire, He passed his mantel on to Elisha, and when King David died, his throne passed onto Solomon, his son, who became king over Israel. Lastly, when Our Lord Jesus was concluding his earthly ministry, he called his twelve disciples together, and gave to them power and authority to cure diseases and have dominion over all devils. The devil knows that God always has a witness and a successor to propagate His purpose. Remember that when John the Baptist came, it was written that he came in the spirit of Elijah. It is the Spirit (of Christ in you) that the devil is after. That is why Jesus early on said to the disciples:

"The world cannot hate you; but me it hateth, because I testify of it, that the works thereof are evil." John 7:7

However, after He had taught them the principles of the kingdom of God and made true believers of them through the impartation of the Spirit, He prayed concerning them saying:

"I have given them thy word; and the world hath hated them, because they are not of the world, even as I am not of the world." John 17:14

So here, we see that the disciples, who the world did not previously hate, are now hated because of the life changing word that they received from the Lord. You may be wondering what the relationship is between the word of Christ and the spirit of Christ that I mentioned earlier. Well here is the answer from Christ:

> *"It is the spirit that quickeneth; the flesh profiteth nothing: the words that I speak unto you, they are spirit, and they are life." John 6:63*

God has given you a purpose in life; and the devil is after that purpose. But you see, that purpose is linked to the Word of God that will not return to God empty but will accomplish all of what it was purposed. If you do not allow God's purpose in you to be realized in your life time, it still will not return to God void but will be passed on to another.

> *"For it is written in the book of Psalms, Let his habitation be desolate, and let no man dwell therein: and his bishoprick* (or, office, or, charge) *let another take."*
> *Acts 1:20*

That therefore, is the reason that the devil comes after you. If you think it is personal, think again. I suggest you seek God enough to learn why He has called you, and following that, work to fulfill your call and election in God.

> *"Wherefore the rather, brethren, give diligence to make your calling and election sure: for if ye do these things, ye shall never fall:" 2nd Peter 1:10*

God has given special weapons to every believer, for use in this war, which is against spiritual beings operating in the spiritual realms. This is not about you, or me, or those around us. It is all about Satan, his vices and his tricks and our quest for a victorious life over him. These weapons are supernatural weapons of warfare uniquely designed to ensure victory. I mean guaranteed victory. There is no way that we can rightly use these weapons and not come out victorious. It is just not possible.

Apostle Paul writes to the church saying,

Introduction to Spiritual Warfare

"3 For though we walk in the flesh, we do not war after the flesh:

4 (For the weapons of our warfare are not carnal, but mighty through God to the pulling down of strong holds;)

5 Casting down imaginations, and every high thing that exalteth itself against the knowledge of God, and bringing into captivity every thought to the obedience of Christ;"
2nd *Corinthians 10:3-5*

That is where we would like to stop, but we cannot stop there because none of these will happen until we have a readiness to revenge all disobedience, when our obedience is fulfilled. As it is written:

"6 And having in a readiness to revenge all disobedience, when your obedience is fulfilled." 2nd *Corinthians 10: 6*

In other words, except I have fully submitted myself unto God, and fully emptied myself into Him, when I try to exert this authority over the enemy, he will ask me the same question that he asked the seven sons of Sceva.

"And the evil spirit answered and said, Jesus I know, and Paul I know; but who are ye?" Acts 19:15

Who are you? Each one of us must know the answer to this question. Each one must have his or her own obedience in place. We need to know that it is not about works or words but rather the witness of the Spirit:

"14 For as many as are led by the Spirit of God, they are the sons of God.

15 For ye have not received the spirit of bondage again to fear; but ye have received the Spirit of adoption, whereby we cry, Abba, Father.

16 The Spirit itself beareth witness with our spirit, that we are the children of God:" Romans 8:14-16

This book will challenge you to take your position as one whom God has called to be more than a conqueror. If you think, you are just a conqueror this book will attempt to change your mind because you see, the bible says that you are not just a conqueror but rather more than a conqueror for it is written:

"31 What shall we then say to these things? If God be for us, who can be against us?
32 He that spared not his own Son, but delivered him up for us all, how shall he not with him also freely give us all things?
33 Who shall lay any thing to the charge of God's elect? It is God that justifieth.
34 Who is he that condemneth? It is Christ that died, yea rather, that is risen again, who is even at the right hand of God, who also maketh intercession for us.
35 Who shall separate us from the love of Christ? shall tribulation, or distress, or persecution, or famine, or nakedness, or peril, or sword?
36 As it is written, For thy sake we are killed all the day long; we are accounted as sheep for the slaughter.
37 Nay, in all these things we are more than conquerors through him that loved us." Romans 8:31-37

You will learn about the nature and scope of spiritual warfare. In addition, get to know your enemy, his organization, targets, strategies, and weapons. When the devil comes to attack us, he does not always come in the obvious form. No, he is more subtle than that. It is oftentimes after he has beguiled us, that we realize his true nature. We need to know him so that 'when the wind begins to blow a certain way you can perceive that it is going to rain.' The person next

Introduction to Spiritual Warfare

to you may say how do you know that, and you may answer 'I can smell it in the air'. Those who live around the coasts can usually tell when a front is approaching even when there is no overwhelming evidence. It is for this purpose of discerning the plan of the enemy, what he is trying to do, how he is trying to do it, who he is trying to use and how he is organized, that God has made available to us the "Gift of the discernment of spirits"

You will also learn how to prepare for warfare in the spiritual arena, so that when you fight, you fight not only to win in battles, but also to win the war and ensure victory that lasts. You see, God has guaranteed our victory, if we stand properly on His Word and upon the promises that He has given us. Since He is a God that cannot lie, will not lie, and has no intention to lie, whatever He says, that He will do.

During the construction of our home, my wife and I had to fight against the spirits of greed and corruption that operate in the building, banking and legal industries. Work had stopped at the site because of the bank's refusal to release funds to the builders. The bank refused the release of funds claiming that the builder was overdrawing the funds. We made all efforts to have the builder address the bank's concern but to no avail so we had to end our contract with that builder with the banks approval. Then we worked with the bank to hire another builder. This new builder performed work at the site but was later also refused payment by the bank because of construction liens. For we found out, that our former builder had unjustly placed liens on our home. Because of this, we had to go to court to have the liens removed so that the bank can pay our new builder and have work continue on site. While this was ongoing, after months of making interest payments on the construction loan at a time when there was no work at the site, we stopped our payments. The other reason we withheld our payments was that the bank refused allow us to take out a bond on the lien as is customary while our case was in litigation. This process could have set the lien aside so that the bank would honor its obligation.

This was a very trying time for us as we have never been in a situation like this before. During one of our hearings, the judge ordered us to go to mediation. The judge also ordered us to invite the bank to take part in the mediation. To our surprise, the bank refused stating that they can only be involved if we sue them. Therefore, we had to sue them. At the mediation with the bank, they revealed to us that because we had stopped making our payments, they had not only foreclosed on our home, but had sold it at a loss in a sheriff sale. The bank told us that we had no rights or claim to our house. Following that disclosure, they decided to make us an offer, which our attorney described as a fair offer. That offer was for us to abandon our home and drop our case against the bank so that they would not come against us for their "loss". Of course, we refused that offer. They extended another offer to us. Our attorney described this new offer as the best that the bank could make and strongly advised us to accept it. This second offer was the same as the first except that the bank would pay us an amount that was less than three percent of what we had invested in the project. Again, we rejected their offer.

We decided to share some fundamental truths with our attorney who at this point had made up in his mind that he was going to drop us as clients since we would not take his counsel to surrender our house and take the loss rather than fight the Goliath (Bank) in our war to obtaining our God-given provision. That truth was simple. God had not asked us to give up the house. We made it clear to him that we were neither in love with the house nor unwilling to take the loss

Introduction to Spiritual Warfare

that he was pressing us to take, but that we came this far trusting in our God and would do nothing without His counsel. Our position threw him over the edge causing him to write to the judge to document his decision to drop us as his clients.

That evening, we went to church to pray with our prayer partners, as is often the case. When we got there, the Lord spoke to us and said:

> *"5 Thou shalt not be afraid for the terror by night; nor for the arrow that flieth by day;*
> *6 Nor for the pestilence that walketh in darkness; nor for the destruction that wasteth at noonday.*
> *7 A thousand shall fall at thy side, and ten thousand at thy right hand; but it shall not come nigh thee.*
> *8 Only with thine eyes shalt thou behold and see the reward of the wicked.*
> *9 ¶ Because thou hast made the LORD, which is my refuge, even the most High, thy habitation;*
> *10 There shall no evil befall thee, neither shall any plague come nigh thy dwelling." Psalms 91:5-10*

He continued to tell us that the word has already gone out that it shall not come nigh thee. Furthermore, you will see the thousand that come at you on your left side and the ten thousand that come at your right side but do not be afraid when you see them. The problem He said with many in the church is that we have not learned to stand in the evil day. When we see the enemy come, we move to the left or to the right of the set place where he placed us and in so doing, we run in to the path of the oncoming enemy. However, He continued, if you stand still in the place that I have placed you, the thousand shall fall at thy side and ten thousand at thy right hand; and there shall no evil befall thee, neither shall any plague come nigh thy dwelling. In addition:

> *"13 Thou shalt tread upon the lion and adder: the young lion and the dragon shalt thou trample under feet.*
> *14 Because he hath set his love upon me, therefore will I deliver him: I will set him on high, because he hath known my name.*
> *15 He shall call upon me, and I will answer him: I will be with him in trouble; I will deliver him, and honour him."*
> *Psalms 91:13-15*

After we heard this, we rejoiced in the Lord, for we were confident that when He has declared victory for us, He will fulfill the victory for us. And He did it for us. He reversed all the actions that the bank had taken against us, and today we live in that house. The difficulty is in positioning ourselves in line with His thoughts and purpose for us.

> *"8 But what saith it ? The word is nigh thee, even in thy mouth, and in thy heart: that is, the word of faith, which we preach;*
> *9 That if thou shalt confess with thy mouth the Lord Jesus, and shalt believe in thine heart that God hath raised him from the dead, thou shalt be saved.*
> *10 For with the heart man believeth unto righteousness; and with the mouth confession is made unto salvation.*
> *11 For the scripture saith, Whosoever believeth on him shall not be ashamed." Romans 10:8-11*

Some may have difficulties accepting this statement from a doctrinal point of view. However, you see, it is not saying that you should not be baptized in Jesus' Name, neither is it saying that you should not be filled with the Holy Ghost. But, after I've been baptized with water and the Holy Ghost then what? Am I supposed to stop believing? Am I supposed to stop worshipping? Am I supposed to stop professing Christ? Am I supposed to stop witnessing? The devil is a liar! That is when you begin to confess Christ Jesus as Lord of your life. It

Introduction to Spiritual Warfare

is after you have fulfilled "your obedience" to the will of God concerning you that you earn the right to exercise your God given weapon for spiritual warfare, which He has uniquely designed to ensure your victory.

"6 And having in a readiness to revenge all disobedience, when your obedience is fulfilled." 2nd Corinthians 10: 6

Recall, when Jesus went to River Jordan to be baptized by John the Baptist, that John recognizing Jesus for who he is, forbad Him saying I am the one who needs baptism and you are the one who should be baptizing me. However, Jesus said no, rather let it be so now that you baptize me, because it is our duty and responsibility to "fulfill all righteousness".

We have to be obedient to fulfill God's plan for our salvation. It is His desire that as many as believe in Him, be baptized in water, calling on the name of the Lord Jesus Christ. It is His desire also that we are baptized with the Holy Spirit, for this is His promise to all who are called by Him. It is after this "righteousness" is fulfilled that we can receive the authority of the believer, and can then with boldness, confess Christ with our mouth. That is why Jesus said to the disciples:

"49 And, behold, I send the promise of my Father upon you: but tarry ye in the city of Jerusalem, until ye be endued with power from on high." Luke 24:49

"4 And, (Jesus) being assembled together with them, commanded them that they should not depart from Jerusalem, but wait for the promise of the Father, which, saith he, ye have heard of me. 5 For John truly baptized with water; but ye shall be baptized with the Holy Ghost not many days hence." Acts 1:4-5

"8 But ye shall receive power, after that the Holy Ghost is come upon you: and ye shall be witnesses unto me both

in Jerusalem, and in all Judaea, and in Samaria, and unto the uttermost part of the earth." Acts 1:8

The other side of that scripture is that if you believe in the Lord Jesus Christ with your entire mind, with all of your heart and with all of your soul, He will see to it that you receive the salvation of your soul. He does that by sending someone your way (as with Philip and the Ethiopian Eunuch, Peter and Cornelius, Aquila and Pricilla and Apollos) to expound the way of God perfectly to you. For a reader of this book today, I am that "someone" that is sent by God to help you become perfectly aligned with the Word of God so that He can release His mighty power to work in your life.

This book is for every believer who aspires to live a victorious Christian life. If that is what you desire, this book will help point to the way, because I believe that my God will supply your needs as He ministers to your Spirit while you read this book. I believe that my God will grant you the desires of your heart as you align yourself to Him. I believe that my God will elevate you spiritually to the place that you should be in Him, and when you reach that place, He will give you the unction to teach and to draw other people to the grace and power of our God, which is in Christ Jesus our LORD.

You are reading this book, I believe, by the divine appointment of God, to help position you, for use by Him in a greater way in other areas of your life. He wants to use you in your work place, in your home and in any other place that He would send you. As you walk with Him, expect to receive from Him, because He has promised to give you "every place that the sole of your feet touches". However, when He gives you "the place", He expects you to subdue it and exercise your dominion over it. AMEN.

WAKE UP OH SLEEPING GIANT

Awake oh Sleeping Giant. Right about now, you are saying, "Do not call me a giant; you do not know where I have been. You do not know how my life has been. You do not know what I have suffered in my life. In addition, you do not know the struggles that I have even now, in my life." However, God has admonished us to cast all our care upon Christ Jesus because he cares for us. When Paul found himself in a similar situation, he wrote:

"8 For this thing I besought the Lord thrice, that it might depart from me.

9 And he said unto me, My grace is sufficient for thee: for my strength is made perfect in weakness. Most gladly therefore will I rather glory in my infirmities, that the power of Christ may rest upon me.

10 Therefore I take pleasure in infirmities, in reproaches, in necessities, in persecutions, in distresses for Christ's sake: for when I am weak, then am I strong."

2nd Corinthians 12:8-10

In other words, God shows out when we are weak. The problem is, often when we are weak; we do not like to approach Him. You see, I believe that the biggest problem with Adam and Eve was not that they ate the forbidden fruit, which of itself was a grievous sin of disobedience. Their bigger problem I believe was that after they ate it, they tried to hide themselves from God. Still, God came looking for them while they were in hiding. If God's intention was to destroy them, He would not have taken the time to cloth them. If it were His intention to kill Cain, who had murdered his brother Abel, He would not have put the mark upon him to protect him from those who could hurt him.

Said differently, because we are children of God, no matter where we are in life, God's will concerning us is that we live and not die. When the Children of Israel left the land of Egypt, they found themselves in the wilderness where for forty years they murmured, complained, and rebelled against the God of their salvation. However, because of His mercy, He continued to guide them and deliver them from the hands of their enemies. Yet he would not let them go into the promise land while their sins remained. But, required of them to turn and take their journey toward the set place – the land of promise.

"6 The LORD our God spake unto us in Horeb, saying, Ye have dwelt long enough in this mount:

7 Turn you, and take your journey, and go to the mount of the Amorites, and unto all the places nigh thereunto, in the plain, in the hills, and in the vale, and in the south, and by the sea side, to the land of the Canaanites, and unto Lebanon, unto the great river, the river Euphrates.

8 Behold, I have set the land before you: go in and possess the land which the LORD sware unto your fathers,

Abraham, Isaac, and Jacob, to give unto them and to their seed after them." Deut. 1:6-8

Therefore, I say to you, lay a memorial where you are, independent of where you may find yourself at this moment. Turn as the Lord has commanded you and take your walk toward God's promises for you, as His Spirit leads you.

THE STATE OF THE CHURCH – THE CALLED

I want to draw your attention to the state of the Church, which is the body of Christ, because you see, when we receive Christ as our Lord and Savior, and follow through with the experience of the new birth as outlined by Christ Himself, we are born into the kingdom of God and into His body. When Nicodemus went to Jesus in search of the way into the Kingdom of God,

> *"3 Jesus answered and said unto him, Verily, verily, I say unto thee, Except a man be born again, he cannot see the kingdom of God.*
>
> *4 Nicodemus saith unto him, How can a man be born when he is old? can he enter the second time into his mother's womb, and be born?*
>
> *5 Jesus answered, Verily, verily, I say unto thee, Except a man be born of water and of the Spirit, he cannot enter into the kingdom of God.*
>
> *6 That which is born of the flesh is flesh; and that which is born of the Spirit is spirit.*
>
> *7 Marvel not that I said unto thee, Ye must be born again."*
>
> *(John. 3:3-7)*

Although we may join a local assembly in order to have fellowship with the brethren, we are members in particular of the body of Christ.

Isaiah wrote:

> *"16 LORD, in trouble have they visited thee, they poured out a prayer when thy chastening was upon them."*
>
> *Isaiah.26:16*

It is a generally known fact that a majority of Christians do not pray consistently when all is well. In fact, many professing Christians do not have dedicated anointed prayer life, consisting of prayer offered independent of current prevailing circumstances. It is particularly sad to note also that some of those who do pray offer no more than a "pop corn" prayer. Nevertheless, we thank God for the remnants, who pray when all is well and when they are faced with life's challenges. However, because of our complacent nature pertaining to our relationship with God, we often find ourselves brushing up against obstacles. These obstacles tend to cause us to remember the name of the Lord our God. It is as though God is saying, "You do not know what I called you to do. You do not know why I called you. I did not call you to live an idle and powerless life. I called you so you can get in position of authority and control. Therefore, I will allow things to come into your life that will cause you, like the prodigal son, to remember your source and origin, as well as who you are in Christ."

> *"17 Like as a woman with child, that draweth near the time of her delivery, is in pain, and crieth out in her pangs; so have we been in thy sight, O LORD."*
>
> *Isaiah 26: 17*

Wake Up Oh Sleeping Giant

I am not a woman, but I was in the delivery room when my children were born. As an observer, I know that there is pain in the delivery process. It is an obvious fact that the pain intensifies as the time of birth draws nearer. The body of Christ is at the point of birth. A greater refreshing of the Spirit of God as has not been seen before is about to take place. God's aim for this outpouring of His Spirit is to empower the believers to live victorious Christian life in this generation. There is a birthing that is about to take place, the only problem is that the Church is asleep.

There is an African expression that says "God forbid that a woman should fall asleep during her labor of child birth" but that is exactly what some in the church have done. This is not the first time that the Church has slumbered. Neither is it the first time we have not been watchful at a critical time when God is ushering in a significant event in the history of the Church.

For you see Jesus Himself found His called out disciples sleeping in the garden of Gethsemane just before His betrayal, and again He found the same bunch fishing when they should be looking for the resurrected Savior. Now, He comes to bestow to the Church, spiritual gifts, power, and authority over our adversary, but this giant is again sleeping. While the people of God are battling identity crisis, not coming to grasp with the power in the finished work of Christ, while we do not appear to know whose Sons we really are, Satan is walking back and forth in the vineyard

> **The body of Christ is at the point of birth, and of a greater refreshing of the Spirit of God like never before, aimed at empowering the believers for victorious Christian life in this generation.**

of God having a field day and ransacking everything over which God has given us dominion.

> *"18 We have been with child, we have been in pain, we have as it were brought forth wind; we have not wrought any deliverance in the earth; neither have the inhabitants of the world fallen." Isaiah 26: 18*

Many of us have not done what God expects of us. Although we know that we are not of "the world", we have become side tracked and drawn by the lures of life to become conformed to our environment. Yet still He admonishes us to:

> *"2 ... be not conformed to this world: but be ye transformed by the renewing of your mind, that ye may prove what is that good, and acceptable, and perfect, will of God." Ro 12:2*

You see, when God called us out of darkness into His marvelous light; it was with the expectation that we would walk in dominion in the earth, and execute deliverance in the earth. Jesus said,

> *"18 The Spirit of the Lord is upon Me, Because He has anointed Me To preach the gospel to the poor; He has sent Me to heal the brokenhearted, To proclaim liberty to the captives And recovery of sight to the blind, To set at liberty those who are oppressed;*
>
> *19 To proclaim the acceptable year of the Lord"*
>
> *Luke 4:18-19 (NKJV)*

Oh, just in case you are thinking that only Jesus alone can have such anointing and power, this is what He said to the disciples that He sent on a mission.

> *"17 Then the seventy returned with joy, saying, 'Lord, even the demons are subject to us in Your name.'*

Wake Up Oh Sleeping Giant

18 And He said to them, 'I saw Satan fall like lightning from heaven.

19 Behold, I give you the authority to trample on serpents and scorpions, and over all the power of the enemy, and nothing shall by any means hurt you'."

Luke 10:17-19 (NKJV)

In addition, if you think this was just for the seventy, listen to what He told His disciples just before He ascended in to heaven:

"16 He that believeth and is baptized shall be saved; but he that believeth not shall be damned.

17 And these signs shall follow them that believe; In my name shall they cast out devils; they shall speak with new tongues;

18 They shall take up serpents; and if they drink any deadly thing, it shall not hurt them; they shall lay hands on the sick, and they shall recover." Mark 16:16-18

God has called us to execute deliverance in the earth. Yet we see the world growing in boldness and gross disregard of the truth, perhaps because very often the church does not mention the Name of the Lord our God. In so doing, we conceal whose we are and for whom we stand. On the other hand, maybe the world is getting bolder and disregarding the truth, because instead of having our lanterns trimmed, so that our light can overpower the darkness around us, we have devised ways to shed our light in the name of "Political Correctness".

Although we have slumbered often, the word declares:

"..., Awake thou that sleepest, and arise from the dead, and Christ shall give thee light". Ephesians 5:14

Moreover, God says:

> *"19 Thy dead men shall live, together with my dead body shall they arise. Awake and sing, ye that dwell in dust: for thy dew is as the dew of herbs, and the earth shall cast out the dead." Isaiah 26: 19*

In other words, God is saying to us, I will restore strength to your weary soul. Furthermore, as you make me the head of your life, I will manifest my strength in you during your weakest moments. As you allow God to arise in your life so will you also be able to rise above your adversaries. Please understand that your unwillingness to enthrone Him over your life does not stop him from being King of kings and Lord of lords. For after Christ was arisen, for Thomas who did not believe, Jesus was not his Lord and his God, yet Jesus Christ was still Lord of lords. However, the moment Thomas had his personal experience and encounter with Christ; he called Him "my Lord and my God." From that time on, for Thomas, He was alive. For you, this may be that moment of personal experience with Jesus Christ when he also becomes your Lord and your God.

Today, God is saying, "Thy dead men shall live". The word 'Men' as used here represents the position of power and authority. He says your dead men shall live, in other words, when you allow me to arise in your life, I will restore back to you, all the power, authority and dominion that I had given you. So,

> *"6 As ye have therefore received Christ Jesus the Lord, so walk ye in him:*
> *7 Rooted and built up in him, and stablished in the faith, as ye have been taught, abounding therein with thanksgiving.*

Wake Up Oh Sleeping Giant

8 Beware lest any man spoil you through philosophy and vain deceit, after the tradition of men, after the rudiments of the world, and not after Christ." Colossians 2:6-8

Therefore, wake up and sing even though you may think that all is lost. Wake up and reject the spirit of bondage that binds us through the cares and struggles of this life. For He says, "Even though your situation is dire and you are feeling completely overpowered, as though you were dead and asleep today, as the morning dew refreshes and gives life to the grass, so will I restore you and refresh you by my Spirit." Wake up He says and:

"20 Come, my people, enter thou into thy chambers, and shut thy doors about thee: hide thyself as it were for a little moment, until the indignation be overpast."

Isaiah 26:20

God's intent is for us to hide in His secret place. If we are going to be a part of this move of the Holy Spirit, we must learn how to hide in His secret place. God does not want His people out in the battle without adequate preparation. He does not want us running ahead of Him. Instead, He wants us to walk in locked step, with His Spirit, which He said should lead us:

"49 And, behold, I send the promise of my Father upon you: but tarry ye in the city of Jerusalem, until ye be endued with power from on high." Luke 24:49

The fathers of the Church were required to move according to the timing of God but we find in the Church today, many who fall on the edge of the sword because they do not know how to wait until the indignation has passed over or till their season of training is ended. We are eager to run for God and that is good. However, in this season, God may want you awake, nurtured by His Word, observant, but sheltered until the season for the manifestation of your God given purpose and destiny. Paul had to go through this process. He spent about three years in the wilderness of Arabia in preparation before Barnabas presented him to the Elders in Jerusalem. In the case of Jesus we read:

> *"13 And when they were departed, behold, the angel of the Lord appeareth to Joseph in a dream, saying, Arise, and take the young child and his mother, and flee into Egypt, and be thou there until I bring thee word: for Herod will seek the young child to destroy him.*
> *14 When he arose, he took the young child and his mother by night, and departed into Egypt:*
> *15 And was there until the death of Herod: that it might be fulfilled which was spoken of the Lord by the prophet, saying, Out of Egypt have I called my son."*
>
> *Matthew 2:13-15*

Many of us are sitting in hiding, waiting for the manifestation of the power of God and the season of that manifestation. For those I say, hold on to the promises of God, for He has declared:

> *"32 And it shall come to pass, that whosoever shall call on the name of the LORD shall be delivered: for in mount Zion and in Jerusalem shall be deliverance, as the LORD hath said, and in the remnant whom the LORD shall call."*
>
> *Joel 2:32*

Therefore, He says wait until I move that indignation. Wait until I move every high thing that stands between you and your purpose. Wait, until I elevate you and strengthen you while you are yet hiding in your nest. Wait until I make you mature by feeding you with my Word and writing it

> **God does not want His people out in the battle without adequate preparation. He does not want us running ahead of Him. Instead, He wants us to walk in locked step with His Spirit, which He said should lead us.**

Wake Up Oh Sleeping Giant

on your heart.

"That in the ages to come he might shew the exceeding riches of his grace in his kindness toward us through Christ Jesus." Eph 2:7

It is after God has restored you as He did with Peter that He should endue you with His power.

" Awake, awake; put on thy strength, O Zion; put on thy beautiful garments, O Jerusalem, the holy city: for henceforth there shall no more come into thee the uncircumcised and the unclean." Isaiah 52:1

It is time for a thorough house cleaning and God himself will do this. He will begin with the Church through the renewing of the inner man as He separates it unto Himself. Put on therefore, your beautiful garments, if you believe in His Name, and adorn yourself as the bride of Christ.

"11 And that, knowing the time, that now it is high time to awake out of sleep: for now is our salvation nearer than when we believed.
12 The night is far spent, the day is at hand: let us therefore cast off the works of darkness, and let us put on the armour of light.
13 Let us walk honestly, as in the day; not in rioting and drunkenness, not in chambering and wantonness, not in strife and envying.
14 But put ye on the Lord Jesus Christ, and make not provision for the flesh, to fulfil the lusts thereof."
Romans 13:11-14

"14Wherefore he saith, Awake thou that sleepest, and arise from the dead, and Christ shall give thee light.
15 See then that ye walk circumspectly, not as fools, but as wise,
16 Redeeming the time, because the days are evil.

17 Wherefore be ye not unwise, but understanding what the will of the Lord is.
18 And be not drunk with wine, wherein is excess; but be filled with the Spirit;" Ephesians 5:14-18

THE STATE OF THE CHURCH – THE LEADERS

Isaiah chapter 25 gives a summary of the state of Israel as a people, who had abandoned their Lord and Deliverer, and become tangled in their sins, brought about by their acts of disobedience and spiritual adultery. Although called to be separate, they found themselves inter-marrying with those that they were supposed to subdue and thus becoming unequally yoked with them. In many ways, the Church, which is the Spiritual Israel, has behaved just like the nation of Israel and their Priests have been alike.

"13 Therefore my people are gone into captivity, because they have no knowledge: and their honourable men are famished, and their multitude dried up with thirst.
14 Therefore hell hath enlarged herself, and opened her mouth without measure: and their glory, and their multitude, and their pomp, and he that rejoiceth, shall descend into it." Isaiah 5:13-14

Ezekiel chapter 22 addresses the state of the priesthood and the leaders of Israel.

"23 And the word of the LORD came unto me, saying, 24 Son of man, say unto her, Thou art the land that is not cleansed, nor rained upon in the day of indignation."
Ezekiel 22:24

The day of indignation represents the days of suffering and pestilence, when things come upon you in an unbearable manner. During this period in your life, you may start speaking to yourself and saying, "wait a minute, this can't happen to me. I am a child of God and I am born again." During this time, you will find that the flow of God's provision tends to be limited. Please note that God's provision is not just material things, as some tend to think, but it does include the fruit of the spirit. As a garden cannot flourish without water, those in this state are also spiritually fruitless. You see, as I have already said, limiting the flow of God's provisions is not about limits to natural means but particularly the spiritual means. It includes those things that tend to increase the quality of our lives, as well as the power to be victorious in our walk with God. Over the decades, we have witnessed many great ministers of the gospel fall, not because of lack of material wealth, but because they failed to allow the favor of the Holy Spirit to make them fruitful. For:

"1 A good name is rather to be chosen than great riches, and loving favour rather than silver and gold"
Proverbs 22:1

God begins here to tell us why the church is going through this day of indignation. He tells us that it is partly because there is a "conspiracy" in the church, which is the body of Christ. He says that:

"25 There is a conspiracy of her prophets in the midst thereof, like a roaring lion ravening the prey; they have devoured souls; they have taken the treasure and precious things; they have made her many widows in the midst thereof.
26 Her priests have violated my law, and have profaned mine holy things: they have put no difference between the holy and profane, neither have they shewed difference between the unclean and the clean, and have hid their eyes from my sabbaths, and I am profaned among them."
Ezekiel 22:25-26

In other words, when the flock of God, which He has asked us to feed, comes in to the Church of God, we the servants of God, like our predecessors in the bible, in many ways do drive them out of the church. We make widows out of them by becoming a hindrance to the people of God as they reach for the groom of their souls.

I remember during the early years of my walk with God, that I was a part of a small but very anointed and powerful ministry. Many had come to know God through this ministry. God had also healed many and performed miracles using this group of teenagers.

However, while this was going on, two of the ministers committed fornication with each other, and God did not conceal it, as He did with King David. Hence, the evangelist got pregnant, and I became ashamed to preach the gospel of Jesus Christ. I could not preach or teach the people about God's sustaining power because of the scandal that had spread through out our little community. I just could not handle the embarrassment brought about by my fellow preachers and that led to my spiral spin away from God and to a total abuse of His grace. Before I knew it, I had backslidden. I did not commit the fornication; in fact I was a virgin but I backslid.

Today, many are falling not because they do not trust God but because the actions of the Church leaders are driving them away from the glorious light of Jesus Christ. What have we not heard or read about the Church these days? Are they not those things that ought not to be once named among us, the saints of God but;

"1 It is reported commonly that there is fornication among you, and such fornication as is not so much as named among the Gentiles, that one should have his father's wife." 1Co 5:1

"3 But fornication, and all uncleanness, or covetousness, let it not be once named among you, as becometh saints;"
Ephesians 5:3

Wake Up Oh Sleeping Giant

When God calls us out and makes us His ambassadors, it carries with it, responsibilities. We cannot be God's ambassador and carry ourselves irresponsibly. The high calling of God, which is in Christ Jesus, calls for a transformation of our ways so that we are more like him hence men will see our good works and glorify our God. Yet, we find today in the church, men and women of God living lives unbecoming of the calling and brining condemnation upon themselves and those who defend them.

"19 And this is the condemnation, that light is come into the world, and men loved darkness rather than light, because their deeds were evil." John 3:19

When God was moving mightily in our small ministry, I was conscious of the responsibility that God had given us, and the inherent danger that could result from our inexperience in ministry. Overwhelmed by the success, I went on a fast asking God to take my life before I would ever backslide. Thank God for a deferred answer for otherwise, I would not be writing this book. I did this however, because I did not want to be responsible for leading any of God's little ones astray. It was a sincere prayer, but prayed out of ignorance. In retrospect, I now realize that it would have been wiser to pray like Solomon:

"7 'Now, O LORD my God, you have made your servant king in place of my father David. But I am only a little child and do not know how to carry out my duties.

8 Your servant is here among the people you have chosen, a great people, too numerous to count or number.

9 So give your servant a discerning heart to govern your people and to distinguish between right and wrong. For who is able to govern this great people of yours?'"

1st *Kings 3:7-9 (NIV)*

Since then, I have come to a greater understanding of the fact that God is the only one who can keep us from falling. I have also come to understand that only God can teach us how to lead His people. Today, many shepherds are struggling, trying to find ways to hold the flock of God in their charge together. However, rather than go to God for direction, they have resorted to becoming men pleasers instead of oracles of God. Yet He holds His under-shepherds responsible for His sheep in their care.

As ministers of God, we should raise the standard of holiness in our lives, just as Moses lifted up the serpent in the wilderness, so that those around us can see the God in us. For when we do this, like the children of Israel, this generation would be drawn to Christ and live. Instead, some of us have become corrupt as we seek fame and the praise of men rather than yearn for the overflow of God's anointing. We no longer focus on knowing Him and the power of His resurrection. Many also are not willing to be partakers in the fellowship of His suffering.

Sacred things are no longer sacred in the church. Unbelievers are able to go the church these days just to be entertained and walk out without the least bit of conviction because we have turned the sacred things of God into playthings. The bible tells us that the Lord adds to the church such as should be saved. The people were baptized in the Name of Jesus Christ as He added them to the church. In addition, God filled them with the Holy Ghost. Is this happening in your fold?

We have allowed things that are sacred such as water baptism, baptism and infilling of the Holy Ghost, the holy communion, the cups and even the furniture in the house of God to be made common. The fact that the veil is torn does not make the sacred things common. The price was excruciating. His sweat was as it were great drops of blood falling down to the ground. Whipping, crown of thorn, public disgrace, carrying the weight of the cross (our sins), nailing to the cross, and a piercing with a spear, represents only a fraction of the price He paid for the veil to be torn down the middle so we all can gain access to the presence of GOD.

Just because we do not need to have bells tied around our waist when we go into the Holy of Holies as the priests, did in the days of the Old Testament, does not give us the right to do as we please.

"For, brethren, ye have been called unto liberty; only use not liberty for an occasion to the flesh, but by love serve one another." Galatians 5:13

Concerning the rulers of the land, it is written:

"27 Her princes in the midst thereof are like wolves ravening the prey, to shed blood, and to destroy souls, to get dishonest gain." Ezekiel 22:27

All across the globe we read and hear about greed and corruption as those in power oppress the very ones they should protect. Blinded by their pride, they see themselves as being invincible. They have not learned the lessons of history, as was the case with Nebuchadnezzar, the king of Babylon for:

"30 The king spake, and said, Is not this great Babylon, that I have built for the house of the kingdom by the might of my power, and for the honour of my majesty?

31 While the word was in the king's mouth, there fell a voice from heaven, saying, O king Nebuchadnezzar, to thee it is spoken; The kingdom is departed from thee.

32 And they shall drive thee from men, and thy dwelling shall be with the beasts of the field: they shall make thee to eat grass as oxen, and seven times shall pass over thee, until thou know that the most High ruleth in the kingdom of men, and giveth it to whomsoever he will.

33 The same hour was the thing fulfilled upon Nebuchadnezzar: and he was driven from men, and did eat grass as oxen, and his body was wet with the dew of heaven, till his hairs were grown like eagles' feathers, and his nails like birds' claws." Daniel 4:30-33

Today, these rulers are driven from their thrones and political offices by their people because they have neither humbled themselves nor lifted up their eyes and looked to the God of all Heavens who made them rulers over his people.

"8 Because thou hast spoiled many nations, all the remnant of the people shall spoil thee; because of men's blood, and for the violence of the land, of the city, and of all that dwell therein.

9 Woe to him that coveteth an evil covetousness to his house, that he may set his nest on high, that he may be delivered from the power of evil!

10 Thou hast consulted shame to thy house by cutting off many people, and hast sinned against thy soul.

11 For the stone shall cry out of the wall, and the beam out of the timber shall answer it.

12 Woe to him that buildeth a town with blood, and stablisheth a city by iniquity!

13 Behold, is it not of the LORD of hosts that the people shall labour in the very fire, and the people shall weary themselves for very vanity?

14 For the earth shall be filled with the knowledge of the glory of the LORD, as the waters cover the sea."

Habakkuk. 2:8-14

Yet through Daniel, He pleads with his rulers saying:

> *"27 Wherefore, O king, let my counsel be acceptable unto thee, and break off thy sins by righteousness, and thine iniquities by shewing mercy to the poor; if it may be a lengthening of thy tranquillity." Daniel 4:27*

If the ruler of the land will heed this plea, God will seize his anger and affliction and begin his work of restoration. First, we must repent of our sins and return to our God. We must humble ourselves before Him and recognize Him as King of kings and Lord of lords. For Nebuchadnezzar,

> *34 ¶ And at the end of the days I Nebuchadnezzar lifted up mine eyes unto heaven, and mine understanding returned unto me, and I blessed the most High, and I praised and honoured him that liveth for ever, whose dominion is an everlasting dominion, and his kingdom is from generation to generation:*
> *35 And all the inhabitants of the earth are reputed as nothing: and he doeth according to his will in the army of heaven, and among the inhabitants of the earth: and none can stay his hand, or say unto him, What doest thou?*
> *36 At the same time my reason returned unto me; and for the glory of my kingdom, mine honour and brightness returned unto me; and my counsellors and my lords sought unto me; and I was established in my kingdom, and excellent majesty was added unto me.*
> *37 Now I Nebuchadnezzar praise and extol and honour the King of heaven, all whose works are truth, and his ways judgment: and those that walk in pride he is able to abase. Daniel 4:34-37*

The point is that the state of the world and of the church has left a lot to be desired. This is why He said:

> *"30 And I sought for a man among them, that should make up the hedge, and stand in the gap before me for the land, that I should not destroy it: but I found none.*
> *31 Therefore have I poured out mine indignation upon them; I have consumed them with the fire of my wrath: their own way have I recompensed upon their heads, saith the Lord GOD." Ezekiel 22:30-31*

In other words, God is saying, "I was looking for someone. I did not just want to come and rain fire and brimstone on these people. I wanted to find a person among them that would say; 'Is there a cause?' Someone who would say; 'what can I do to help'. Someone that would say; 'send me'. I wanted a prayer warrior. I wanted a soldier that is armed and ready to fight the good warfare of faith but I could not find one so I allowed the people to suffer".

Today, remnant leaders are hearing the cries of the people and wondering what to do. They are seeking ways to go about leading a people who have become so used to suffering that they have forgotten who they are and whose they are.

> *"10 And when Pharaoh drew nigh, the children of Israel lifted up their eyes, and, behold, the Egyptians marched after them; and they were sore afraid: and the children of Israel cried out unto the LORD.*
> *11 And they said unto Moses, Because there were no graves in Egypt, hast thou taken us away to die in the wilderness? wherefore hast thou dealt thus with us, to carry us forth out of Egypt?*
> *12 Is not this the word that we did tell thee in Egypt, saying, Let us alone, that we may serve the Egyptians? For it had been better for us to serve the Egyptians, than that we should die in the wilderness.*
> *13 And Moses said unto the people, Fear ye not, stand still, and see the salvation of the LORD, which he will*

Wake Up Oh Sleeping Giant

shew to you to day: for the Egyptians whom ye have seen to day, ye shall see them again no more for ever.
14 The LORD shall fight for you, and ye shall hold your peace." Exodus 14:10-14

God speaks to those who are willing to make up the hedge and stand in the gap before God for the land: as He did to Moses in the wilderness,

"15 And the LORD said unto Moses, Wherefore criest thou unto me? speak unto the children of Israel, that they go forward:
16 But lift thou up thy rod, and stretch out thine hand over the sea, and divide it: and the children of Israel shall go on dry ground through the midst of the sea.
17 And I, behold, I will harden the hearts of the Egyptians, and they shall follow them: and I will get me honour upon Pharaoh, and upon all his host, upon his chariots, and upon his horsemen.
18 And the Egyptians shall know that I am the LORD, when I have gotten me honour upon Pharaoh, upon his chariots, and upon his horsemen." Exodus 14:15-18

God is working with those who have ears to hear and eyes to see. He is still working things out to His glory. However, He desires a partnership with His shepherds. He requires us to use all the gifts that He has given us to the benefit rather than exploitation of the sheep. As with Ezekiel, He is strategically placing His prophets and priests by the "River of Chebar".

"14 So the spirit lifted me up, and took me away, and I went in bitterness, in the heat of my spirit; but the hand of the LORD was strong upon me.

15 Then I came to them of the captivity at Telabib, that dwelt by the river of Chebar, and I sat where they sat, and remained there astonished among them seven days.

16 And it came to pass at the end of seven days, that the word of the LORD came unto me, saying,
17 Son of man, I have made thee a watchman unto the house of Israel: therefore hear the word at my mouth, and give them warning from me." Ezekiel 2:14-17

Moreover, I can imagine that Ezekiel probably heard them sing the song of slavery:

"1 By the rivers of Babylon, there we sat down, yea, we wept, when we remembered Zion.
2 We hanged our harps upon the willows in the midst thereof.
3 For there they that carried us away captive required of us a song; and they that wasted us required of us mirth, saying, Sing us one of the songs of Zion.
4 How shall we sing the LORD'S song in a strange land?"
Psalms 137: 1 - 4

Like him, we hear the cries and feel the hurts of the people of God as they weep saying.

"4 How shall we sing the LORD'S song in a strange land?
5 If I forget thee, O Jerusalem, let my right hand forget her cunning.
6 If I do not remember thee, let my tongue cleave to the roof of my mouth; if I prefer not Jerusalem above my chief joy." Psalms 137: 4 - 6

As God develops the burden in us, we tend to ask the question "why me? Why am I going through the things that I am going through? Why can I not get the breakthrough that I need even though I have been fasting, praying, and seeking His face?" While you wait, remember the words of Ezekiel:

"15......and I sat where they sat, and remained there astonished among them seven days.
16 And it came to pass at the end of seven days, that the word of the LORD came unto me, saying,"

Wake Up Oh Sleeping Giant

Ezekiel 2:15-16

Be assured that He will speak to you to reveal to you the reason for your travail:

"For the vision is yet for an appointed time, but at the end it shall speak, and not lie: though it tarry, wait for it; because it will surely come, it will not tarry."

Habakkuk. 2:3

"For yet a little while, and he that shall come will come, and will not tarry." Hebrews 10:37

At the end of your "seven days", He will take you to your "Valley of Dry Bones" and will ask you the same question that He asked of Ezekiel, "Son of Man, can these bones live?" You have seen them, heard them, and listened to their conversation. Can they live? Is there any hope left in this people? Is there reason for this people to want to come back to life? Can these bones live?

"1 The hand of the LORD was upon me, and carried me out in the spirit of the LORD, and set me down in the midst of the valley which was full of bones,
2 And caused me to pass by them round about: and, behold, there were very many in the open valley and, lo, they were very dry.
3 And he said unto me, Son of man, can these bones live? And I answered, O Lord GOD, thou knowest."

Ezekiel 37:1-3

Ezekiel was familiar with his responsibility as a Prophet, having been previously instructed how to walk in the office of the prophet.

"1 And he said unto me, Son of man, stand upon thy feet, and I will speak unto thee.
2 And the spirit entered into me when he spake unto me, and set me upon my feet, that I heard him that spake unto me.

3 And he said unto me, Son of man, I send thee to the children of Israel, to a rebellious nation that hath rebelled against me: they and their fathers have transgressed against me, even unto this very day.
4 For they are impudent children and stiffhearted. I do send thee unto them; **and thou shalt say unto them, Thus saith the Lord GOD.**
5 And they, whether they will hear, or whether they will forbear, (for they are a rebellious house,) yet shall know that there hath been a prophet among them."

Ezekiel 2:1-5

Today many in the Church have set the ark of God upon a new cart, by departing from the call of God to preach the Gospel in season and out of season. However, when you remember that you are nothing but a voice, like Ezekiel you will say, *"O Lord GOD, thou knowest"* for I have nothing to say to these bones but what says the LORD. I can imagine God say to him, "If you think that I know their ending, then walk with me, do what I say, and say what I say to these bones." You see with God, it is not just, about what we say but it is also, about how we act. "If you believe that I know the answer, then be my spokesperson and let me operate through you because I have given you dominion in the earth. I want you to echo what I say". We have to be able to speak God's word with conviction.

"4 Again he said unto me, Prophesy upon these bones, and say unto them, O ye dry bones, hear the word of the LORD.
5 Thus saith the Lord GOD unto these bones; Behold, I will cause breath to enter into you, and ye shall live:
6 And I will lay sinews upon you, and will bring up flesh upon you, and cover you with skin, and put breath in you, and ye shall live; and ye shall know that I am the LORD." Ezekiel 37:4-6

Wake Up Oh Sleeping Giant

It sounds ridiculous does it not. We have ears, yet cannot hear, eyes, and yet cannot see, but now we find ourselves in a valley full of dry bones that are not even connected one to another and we are to tell them to hear the Word of God. You see, God sometimes put us in what appears to be an impossible situation but then again it is not about what our eyes can see or how we feel about our circumstance. If we believe in Him, we have to do as He has commanded us. Ezekiel did just that. He did exactly as God commanded him.

> *"7 So I prophesied as I was commanded: and as I prophesied, there was a noise, and behold a shaking, and the bones came together, bone to his bone.*
> *8 And when I beheld, lo, the sinews and the flesh came up upon them, and the skin covered them above: but there was no breath in them." Ezekiel 37:7-8*

In addition, he watched to see every word confirmed. Part of the problem with the church is that we pray without expectation. We ought to watch to see yolks lifted off the people of God and expect to see burdens destroyed as commanded. For the Lord Himself has said:

> *"8 For my thoughts are not your thoughts, neither are your ways my ways, saith the LORD.*
> *9 For as the heavens are higher than the earth, so are my ways higher than your ways, and my thoughts than your thoughts.*
> *10 For as the rain cometh down, and the snow from heaven, and returneth not thither, but watereth the earth, and maketh it bring forth and bud, that it may give seed to the sower, and bread to the eater:*
> *11 So shall my word be that goeth forth out of my mouth: it shall not return unto me void, but it shall accomplish that which I please, and it shall prosper in the thing whereto I sent it." Isaiah 55:8-11*

His word will not come back void. Though it tarry, wait for it, because it will surely come, it will not tarry and at the end, it shall speak and not lie. We should realize that when God sends His word, the devil does also mobilize his forces to fight against the Word. This is why we have to be vigilant as we wait for the fulfillment of the Word of God. Daniel shows us an example of earnest expectation when he prayed concerning the return of Israel.

> **God sometimes put us in what appears to be an impossible situation but then again it is not about what our eyes can see or how we feel about our circumstance. If we believe in Him, we have to do as He has commanded us.**

"2 In the first year of his reign I Daniel understood by books the number of the years, whereof the word of the LORD came to Jeremiah the prophet, that he would accomplish seventy years in the desolations of Jerusalem. 3 And I set my face unto the Lord God, to seek by prayer and supplications, with fasting, and sackcloth, and ashes:" Daniel 9:2, 3

We see however that even with Daniel praying, it took three weeks to get the response from God to Daniel because of the resistance from the "prince of Persia." What should we expect if we do not pray and seek His face of which He has declared:

"14 If my people, which are called by my name, shall humble themselves, and pray, and seek my face, and turn from their wicked ways; then will I hear from heaven, and will forgive their sin, and will heal their land."
2nd *Chronicles 7:14*

Wake Up Oh Sleeping Giant

When we fail to set our faces unto the Lord our God to seek His face by prayer and supplications, with fasting, concerning His promises to us, we cause the promises, which God meant for us to pass unto the next generation. As He did in the wilderness, the unbelief of one generation did not stop the next generation from entering the promise land but it kept that generation of unbelievers from entering into it.

It was after Ezekiel had exacted his obedience and did exactly what God commanded him to do that:

"..., there was a noise, and behold a shaking, and the bones came together, bone to his bone. 8 And when I beheld, lo, the sinews and the flesh came up upon them, and the skin covered them above: but there was no breath in them." Ezekiel 37:7b-8

This brings us to the state of the current day church. You see today, we have the Gospel, which is the good news that God has extended a way unto salvation to whosoever will. We have the doctrines. We have the "people" in place (that is, the Apostles, the Prophets, the Evangelists, the Pastors and the Teachers) for the edification of the Body of Christ. However, some in the Body of Christ; have not perceived the blowing of the wind of God. Because of this lack of sensitivity to the things of the Spirit, many assemblies and denominations are lying dormant like dead men and women. They have become as a valley filled with dead men and women for:

"They profess that they know God; but in works they deny him, being abominable, and disobedient, and unto every good work reprobate". Titus 1:16

Nevertheless, God says, "I will do one more thing. You see up until now, you have been speaking to the things that you can see but now I want you to speak to what you cannot see". It is a progressive faith process. You can use as a foundation, the faith that you exercised when you were dealing with things that you could see. God reveals righteousness from faith to faith as He works with us in a systematic way. First,

> *".....He said unto me, Prophesy upon these bones, and say unto them, O ye dry bones, hear the word of the LORD.*
> *7 So I prophesied as I was commanded: and as I prophesied, there was a noise, and behold a shaking, and the bones came together, bone to his bone.*
> *8 And when I beheld, lo, the sinews and the flesh came up upon them, and the skin covered them above: but there was no breath in them." Ezekiel 37:6-8*

We see here how God builds our faith by sometimes dealing with us in the areas of our senses or familiarity for we can hear a noise, feel the shaking, see the bones coming together, and then the muscles, flesh and skin, coming together but that is only the beginning of our journey into destiny.

To go to where destiny lives, you must speak to things that you cannot see. Having learned that God is able to back up your words with signs and wonders, you must be ready to move to the second level of obedience. This level of obedience, which is born out of faith, does not rely on possibility of the expected outcome, but rather on the certainty of Him in whom you believe. How REAL is GOD to YOU?

> *"9 Then said he unto me, Prophesy unto the wind, prophesy, son of man, and say to the wind, Thus saith the Lord GOD; Come from the four winds, O breath, and breathe upon these slain, that they may live." Ezekiel 37:9*

When you apply the faith that God has built up in you, during your next level of obedience to His command, there

Wake Up Oh Sleeping Giant

will be a noise, but this noise will not be like the first noise. For the first noise was due to the movement of tangible things (bones). However, this second noise will be because of a spiritual move. For this is the same sound spoken of in the day of Pentecost:-

> *"And suddenly there came a sound from heaven as of a rushing mighty wind, and it filled all the house where they were sitting." Acts 2:2*

This Wind is the life giving breath of the MOST HIGH GOD. When we allow God, through our obedience to His Word, to cause His breath, which is His Spirit, to fall upon and into us, He restores order to the dry and lifeless places in our lives. So was the case with these skeletons. Ezekiel said:

> **The next level of obedience is born out of faith. It does not rely on possibility of the expected outcome, but rather on the certainty of Him in whom you believe.**

> *"10 So I prophesied as he commanded me, and the breath came into them, and they lived, and stood up upon their feet, an exceeding great army." Ezekiel 37:10*

Therefore, when I address the church as a sleeping giant, it is in-fact who we are. However, for now, the bible says that we say that our hope is gone.

> *"11 Then he said unto me, Son of man, these bones are the whole house of Israel: behold, they say, Our bones are dried, and our hope is lost: we are cut off for our parts."*
> *Ezekiel 37:11*

We say that we are nothing and nobodies, because we are looking at our situations and our circumstances. Although we know in whom we believe, we are not so sure that He can hear us all the time.

Fighting To Win - Volume One

We know that there is no fault in Him. Yet we find it hard to trust Him because of all the faults in us. For these reasons, we limit God, and His desire to save us. So He said to Ezekiel:

> *"12 Therefore prophesy and say unto them, Thus saith the Lord GOD; Behold, O my people, I will open your graves, and cause you to come up out of your graves, and bring you into the land of Israel.*
> *13 And ye shall know that I am the LORD, when I have opened your graves, O my people, and brought you up out of your graves,*
> *14 And shall put my spirit in you, and ye shall live, and I shall place you in your own land: then shall ye know that I the LORD have spoken it, and performed it, saith the LORD." Ezekiel 37:12-14*

What an opportunity to escape from the bondage of sin and of the cares of this life and receive the abundance of God's grace, which He gives freely to us. We know that:

> *"17 Every good gift and every perfect gift is from above, and cometh down from the Father of lights, with whom is no variableness, neither shadow of turning.*
> *18 Of his own will begat he us with the word of truth, that we should be a kind of firstfruits of his creatures."*
> *James 1:17-18*

For, when we could not help ourselves, and when no one would help, He emptied himself and took on the form of a servant, and was made in the likeness of men. He gave His Name to that body calling Him JESUS, which in Hebrew is Jehoshua meaning, "Jehovah is salvation".

> *"11 He came unto his own, and his own received him not.*
> *12 But as many as received him, to them he gave the power to become the sons of God, even to them that believe on his name:*

Wake Up Oh Sleeping Giant

13 Which were born, not of blood, nor of the will of the flesh, nor of the will of man, but of God." John 1:11-13

He did not only give us the power to become the sons of God; He also imputed his righteousness on us. In addition, says to us:

"..., All power is given unto me in heaven and in earth."
Matthew 28:18

"1Behold, I give unto you power to tread on serpents and scorpions, and over all the power of the enemy: and nothing shall by any means hurt you." Luke 10:19

"¶ Awake, awake; put on thy strength, O Zion; put on thy beautiful garments, O Jerusalem, the holy city: for henceforth there shall no more come into thee the uncircumcised and the unclean." Isaiah 52:1

"¶ Arise, shine; for thy light is come, and the glory of the LORD is risen upon thee." Isaiah 60:1

Paul wrote to the church to remind us of His intent for us after we have awakened. You see God did not wake us up just to sit and look around. He has awakened us to understand who we are and get back to what we should to be doing.

"11 ¶ And that, knowing the time, that now it is high time to awake out of sleep: for now is our salvation nearer than when we believed.
12 The night is far spent, the day is at hand: let us therefore cast off the works of darkness, and let us put on the armour of light." Romans 13:11-12
"15 See then that ye walk circumspectly, not as fools, but as wise,
16 Redeeming the time, because the days are evil.
17 Wherefore be ye not unwise, but understanding what the will of the Lord is.

18 And be not drunk with wine, wherein is excess; but be filled with the Spirit;" Ephesians 5:15-18

It is like riding a horse, if you fall off the horse, you do not just get up and say, well that was a nice ride, and I am done. Oh no, you are not, because people do not fall off the horse when they reach their destination. Falling off in fact indicates that you have not reached your destination. For when you reach your destination, you will dismount under a controlled sequence. Therefore, should you fall off your horse, get up, climb right back on that horse and continue the course. The same applies to our walk with God.

"14Wherefore he saith, Awake thou that sleepest, and arise from the dead, and Christ shall give thee light."
Ephesians 5:14

Now that God has awakened us from sleep, He wants us to know our position in Him. He also wants us to know who we are in Him. We will rightly adjust our attitude once we know who we are in him. This knowledge will change the way we conduct ourselves and the way we go about doing the things that we do.

Armed with the Word of God and the whole amour of God, let us therefore brethren, take our position as ones who have been called to be more than a conqueror. Let us take back control as we put to an end, every work of darkness. Let us dismantle every high thing that exalts itself against the knowledge of God and bring into captivity every thought to the obedience of Christ. Let us through our obedience; crown Him King of kings and Lord of lords in all aspects of our lives. Let our conduct at all times and in every situation be to the GLORY OF GOD.

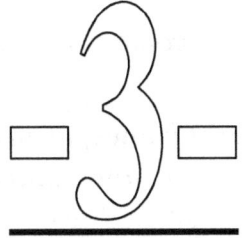

THE BATTLE IN PROGRESS

THE SCOPE OF THE BATTLE

The God, who has called us unto good works through the quickening of His Holy Spirit, requires us, the Body of Christ, to realize that there is a battle in progress. This spiritual warfare is ongoing and calls for us to become aware of its existence, and familiar with its nature and scope. When Isaiah wrote of Israel, God's elect, he said:

> *"22 But this is a people robbed and spoiled; they are all of them snared in holes, and they are hid in prison houses: they are for a prey, and none delivereth; for a spoil, and none saith, Restore." Isaiah 42:22*

Most of us find ourselves in this state today. Just like in the days of Gideon, even though we have obtained God's great promises, we still find ourselves a people robbed and spoiled; snared in holes, hid in prison houses, and ultimately given up as it were, for a prey. All of these things are happening to us because we have not learned to subdue, dominate and take complete control of the things that He has given us, by exercising our God given authority over them. Neither have we learned how to properly fight the fight of faith.

"41 ¶ And when he was come near, he beheld the city, and wept over it,

42 Saying, If thou hadst known, even thou, at least in this thy day, the things which belong unto thy peace! but now they are hid from thine eyes.

43 For the days shall come upon thee, that thine enemies shall cast a trench about thee, and compass thee round, and keep thee in on every side,

44 And shall lay thee even with the ground, and thy children within thee; and they shall not leave in thee one stone upon another; because thou knewest not the time of thy visitation." Luke 19:41-44

When Jesus came near the city of Jerusalem, He looked at it, and began to cry because Jerusalem did not know what God had given to her for her peace and well-being. This ignorance Jesus said, will lead to her desolation. In other words, because of our inability to understand our environment, as with Sampson, events and circumstances in our lives can overtake, weaken and so render us incapable of operating from our position of strength.

This is the time of the visitation of the Spirit of God. He is here, as never before. He has brought with Him prophetic authority, dreams, visions, and yes! Anointing for the deliverance of those bound and afflicted by the enemy. He gives these powers to the remnants, who not only believe on His name, but also dare to call upon the His name. For the word declares:

"28 ¶ And it shall come to pass afterward, that I will pour out my spirit upon all flesh; and your sons and your daughters shall prophesy, your old men shall dream dreams, your young men shall see visions:" Joel 2:28

The Battle in Progress

"32 And it shall come to pass, that whosoever shall call on the name of the LORD shall be delivered: for in mount Zion and in Jerusalem shall be deliverance, as the LORD hath said, and in the remnant whom the LORD shall call."

Joel 2:32

It is very important that we know that this is a spiritual battle:

"3For though we walk in the flesh, we do not war after the flesh:" 2nd Corinthians 10:3

This is not a flesh (physical) encounter, neither is it about people going at each other. No, this battle is not about that, for all that is of the flesh is only temporal but this battle seeks to inflict a more permanent damage on the body of Christ and its members. Recognizing his participation in the ongoing warfare, Paul writes:

"¶ For, when we were come into Macedonia, our flesh had no rest, but we were troubled on every side; without were fightings, within were fears." 1st Corinthians 7:5

This therefore teaches us that spiritual warfare takes place both on the outside and on the inside of the believer. I want to address for a moment the external and internal wars. We will find that although the conditions of the battle, as well as where the battle takes place may be different; the results of these occurrences are the same.

THE STRUGGLES WITHIN

In the late 1960s through 1970, there was a civil war in Nigeria. For those who may not know, Nigeria is one of the largest and most thickly populated countries in Africa. It is very rich in culture and mineral resources. Her rich culture originates from her indigenous tribal states.

These tribes were grouped together to form the Northern and the Southern Protectorates by their colonial master during the period of the scramble and partitioning of Africa. In 1914, the colonial master amalgamated these Protectorates to create a new country called Nigeria, a name derived from River Niger, the principal river that flows through the land. This brief lesson on Nigeria is actually quite similar to the experience of many Christians. For as Nigeria is made up of these different indigenous tribes, so is the Christian made up of the Natural and the Spiritual natures. As Nigerians, work to create a country not only in name but one also unified in a sense of purpose, so do Christians strive to bring all aspects of their life under subjection to the will and purpose of God.

> **The Internal War**
> **- The Nigerian Experience -**
> **Effect at the War Front:**
> - Destruction (death)
> - Physical handicap or disablement
> - Mental handicap or diminished will to fight
>
> **Reasons:**
> - Well known by the enemy – culture, spirit and will
> - Familiar territory (Physical Characteristics)
> - No hiding place
>
> **Impact at Home:**
> - Imprisoned at Home
> - Refugee at Home
> - Starvation at Home
> - Restlessness at Home
> - Low moral
> - Increased acts of disobedience
> - Weakened faith
> - Sense of hopelessness

Moreover, as political, social, and economic tensions lead to national unrest in Nigeria, as a result ideological differences among the native tribes, so do Christians find within themselves, internal conflict, as the fruit of the Spirit and the works of the flesh battle for control of the Christian's

The Battle in Progress

life.

> *"16 This I say then, Walk in the Spirit, and ye shall not fulfil the lust of the flesh.*
>
> *17 For the flesh lusteth against the Spirit, and the Spirit against the flesh: and these are contrary the one to the other: so that ye cannot do the things that ye would."*
> Galatians 5:16-17

We find in general, that the ingredients for internal battle are home made. There is usually no third party involvement, but the individual alone, having a battle within. When Paul found himself in this state, he wrote:

> *"21 I find then a law, that, when I would do good, evil is present with me.*
>
> *22 For I delight in the law of God after the inward man:*
>
> *23 But I see another law in my members, warring against the law of my mind, and bringing me into captivity to the law of sin which is in my members." Romans 7:21-23*

In the case of the Nigerian civil war, the results at the war front were destruction (death), physical handicap or disablement, mental handicap and a diminished will to fight. One thing is evident, where there is war, whether civil or an internal spiritual battle, there will be some casualty. No one goes to war and returns without a mental or psychological change. In addition to physical death, war kills emotionally. It also kills dreams and destroys families. Every war destroys some life. Every war maims someone, and yes, someone will lose the will to go on because of the war. However, it need not be the child of God for we must remember these words of our Father as he says to us:

> *"1 ¶ When thou goest out to battle against thine enemies, and seest horses, and chariots, and a people more than*

thou, be not afraid of them: for the LORD thy God is with thee, which brought thee up out of the land of Egypt."
Deuteronomy 20:1

There are several reasons for the devastations, which the people experienced during the Nigerian civil war.
First, the people that we called our enemies knew us very well. They had been our neighbors for centuries. After generations of inter migration of families from cities in one tribe to cities in other tribes, the immigrant families knew each other's culture, spirit and will, because they lived among each other. In other words, they knew certain things that one was capable of doing and those things that one could not do.

Second, since they were in a familiar territory, there were no surprises lying in wait for them. For instance, they were familiar with the seasons and climates as well as the changes in our life style due to seasonal changes.

Third, because of the in-depth knowledge of each other and familiarity with each other's ways, there was no hiding place for either side. Those were the ingredients for the high degree of casualty that resulted from the Nigerian Civil War. For our internal struggles, the devil knows our fears and our trepidations. He knows our strengths, weaknesses and the fights we do not want to fight.

While the struggles of the 1960s may have been due to ethnic tensions, in 2011, Nigeria found itself dealing with internal struggles. This time, the issues appear to be a religious divide. Nigeria's population of more than 160 million people consist mainly Muslim to the north and predominantly Christian to the south, although followers of both faiths have co-existed for years in the different regions. In recent years, a group believed to have a number of factions with differing aims,

The Battle in Progress

including a hard-core Islamist wing named "Boko Haram", which means, "Western education is forbidden", began its insurgent activities against Christian establishments in the North. The attacks on Christians led to the killing many innocent people, and sparked fears of a wider religious conflict.

Nigerian President Goodluck Jonathan said that violence blamed on Boko Haram was worse than the 1960s civil war. "The situation we have in our hands is even worse than the civil war that we fought," Jonathan said. "During the civil war, we knew and we could even predict where the enemy was coming from ... But the challenge we have today is more complicated." Jonathan said. Boko Haram members and sympathizers could be found throughout society, "Some of them are in the executive arm of government, some of them are in the parliamentary and legislative arm of government, while some of them are even in the judiciary," he said. "Some are also in the armed forces, the police and other security agencies. Some continue to dip their hands and eat with you and you won't even know the person who will point a gun at you or plant a bomb behind your house," he said.

We should clearly note the effect of the civil war or unrest on the general population, as it exemplifies what can happen to us as we deal with fears within. For though at home, where freedom should abound, fear and prevailing uncertainties about the future, imprisoned the people. There was a great disruption of normal lifestyle. Most people eliminated long-term plans because the owners of the land had become refugees at home. Without stability, agricultural development became limited and steadily led to starvation, restlessness, low morale and increased acts of disobedience for "a hungry person is an angry person". Faith and courage gave way to frustration and a growing sense of hopelessness. All of these things were side effects of ongoing internal war that was in progress.

The question is; what should children of God do when they have to face the fears that lurk within? Do the first things first. Look within and examine yourself to make sure that you are in right standing with God. People claim to be innocent until proven guilty. If we honestly look into the perfect mirror, which is the Word of God, His Spirit, which dwells within us, will "prove" our innocence or guilt. It is only then that we can know whether we have given place to the devil by breaking our covenant with God and revolting against His law. For;

> *"20 If I justify myself, mine own mouth shall condemn me: if I say, I am perfect, it shall also prove me perverse."*
> *Job 9:20*

> *"20 For if our heart condemn us, God is greater than our heart, and knoweth all things.*
>
> *21 Beloved, if our heart condemn us not, then have we confidence toward God." 1John 3:20-21*

> *"9 If we confess our sins, he is faithful and just to forgive us our sins, and to cleanse us from all unrighteousness."*
> *1John 1:9*

When we look at ourselves, recognize and take responsibility for our fault, and ask God's forgiveness He will forgive our sins and remove all records of our offenses. In addition, like a loving father, He will correct us and set us back on the right path. We should always remember that:

"12 The night is far spent, the day is at hand: let us therefore cast off the works of darkness, and let us put on the armour of light.

The Battle in Progress

13 Let us walk honestly, as in the day; not in rioting and drunkenness, not in chambering and wantonness, not in strife and envying.

14 But put ye on the Lord Jesus Christ, and make not provision for the flesh, to fulfil the lusts thereof."
Romans 13:12-14

We have already heard from Paul that in a state of internal struggle, it is difficult to do the things we know are right. Peter therefore points us to the way to victory. He reminds us that we are:

"4[Born anew] into an inheritance which is beyond the reach of change and decay [imperishable], unsullied and unfading, reserved in heaven for you,

5 Who are being guarded (garrisoned) by God's power through [your] faith [till you fully inherit that [final] salvation that is ready to be revealed [for you] in the last time.

6[You should] be exceedingly glad on this account, though now for a little while you may be distressed by trials and suffer temptations,

7 So that [the genuineness] of your faith may be tested, [your faith] which is infinitely more precious than the perishable gold which is tested and purified by fire. [This proving of your faith is intended] to redound to [your] praise and glory and honor when Jesus Christ (the Messiah, the Anointed One) is revealed." 1st Peter 1:4-7 (Amplified)

God's desire is that we leave no room for the enemy. Our Lord Jesus Christ said that the prince of this world had nothing in Him. If Satan could not get in and corrupt the mind of Christ, he should not be able to corrupt his body.

"13So brace up your minds; be sober (circumspect, morally alert); set your hope wholly and unchangeably on the grace (divine favor) that is coming to you when Jesus Christ (the Messiah) is revealed.

14[Live] as children of obedience [to God]; do not conform yourselves to the evil desires [that governed you] in your former ignorance [when you did not know the requirements of the Gospel].

15But as the One Who called you is holy, you yourselves also be holy in all your conduct and manner of living."

1st *Peter 1:13-15* (Amplified)

THE EXTERNAL WAR

Now let us consider the international or external war. In an effort to thwart the spread of communism into Vietnam and surrounding countries, the United States found itself gradually drawn into a foreign war that would last about fifteen years. As perhaps seen by President John Fitzgerald Kennedy, this war would be to insure the survival and the success of liberty and for this cause he declared "...we shall pay any price, bear any burden, meet any hardship, support any friend, oppose any foe, to insure the survival and the success of liberty." What may have eluded the United States (US) was that the mindset of the North Vietnamese government was to fight for, and unite Vietnam as one communist country at all cost.

History tells us that the ensuing Vietnam War stands to date as the longest war in American History. That alone is not surprising, for history is also full of wars that have lasted considerably longer. The surprise however, lies in the fact that not only could the peasant Vietnamese enemy engage the US for about fifteen years, but also would also win the war

The Battle in Progress

despite the overwhelming advantage in size and conventional strength by super power US.

During the years of fighting in a foreign land, the American troops experienced many things. Principal among their experiences was the death of fellow compatriots in combat, as over 55,000 Americans lost their life due to this war. Secondly, they experienced physical handicap or disablement. For hundreds of thousands of Americans returned home from this war wounded while yet thousands more came home maimed for life.

In addition to the physical wounds, there were also cases of mental and psychological wounds. When the war ended, more than two thousand Americans were missing in action, held prisoners of war, or brought home for treatment in our mental institutions

Why would a third world country, inflict so much pain on the mightier United States? Well, let me propose the following rather simplistic reasons.

First, the enemy was unknown. As with any guerrilla warfare, the identity of the guerrilla warriors was unknown, as were also their plans and tactics.

Second, the war was in a foreign land, which was also an unfamiliar environment. The enemy in this case was

---

The External War
- The Vietnam Experience -

Effect at the War Front:
- Destruction (death)
- Physical handicap or disablement
- Mental handicap or diminished will to fight

Reasons:
- Unknown enemy
- Unfamiliar territory (Physical Characteristics)
- The "little foxes" – culture, spirit and will

Impact at Home:
- Low moral
- Increased acts of disobedience
- Weakened faith
- Sense of hopelessness

fighting at home.

They knew the locations of the natural dangers and used them to their advantage. They were able to disguise as local farmers when necessary to escape the wrath of the US. Third, they had a language advantage for they could speak the local language, an attribute, which enabled them to hide from not only the US soldiers but also the locals who supported the US.

Fourth, the factor that I call the "little foxes" also contributed to Americas' pain and misery. These "little foxes" included the culture of the people, their beliefs, their courage and the level to which they were committed to fight. Other than these "little foxes", the Vietnamese would not stand a chance against the United States of America. We need to know the intangible facts about our enemy such as its nature, its drive, and its resiliency. Failures to know such will usually present a significant challenge and limit any predictions of victory.

Spiritual warfare is not an emotional warfare. The stakes are high as are the cost. We should not allow the enemy to lure us into war. Our enemy knows that when our focus is on Christ, our victory is certain. Therefore, he resorts to a "guerrilla warfare" approach. He does this by starting the attack and then running to his position of strength hoping to draw us from our position of strength as we pursue him. If we should fall prey to his trick and pursue him into his territory, we would then expose ourselves to unfamiliar situations. When one finds oneself in an unfamiliar situation, it is common to experience a decrease in confidence with every increase in uncertainty. The more uncertain things become, the greater the potential to doubt. As doubt increases, so faith also decreases. Our confidence however, is in our God.

The Battle in Progress

"For in him we live, and move, and have our being; as certain also of your own poets have said, For we are also his offspring" Acts 17:28

David the king clearly showed us how to handle an attack of the enemy which aims at drawing us into an external conflict: Here is his story:

" 1 Now it happened, when David and his men came to Ziklag, on the third day, that the Amalekites had invaded the South and Ziklag, attacked Ziklag and burned it with fire,

2 and had taken captive the women and those who were there, from small to great; they did not kill anyone, but carried them away and went their way.

3 So David and his men came to the city, and there it was, burned with fire; and their wives, their sons, and their daughters had been taken captive.

4 Then David and the people who were with him lifted up their voices and wept, until they had no more power to weep.

5 And David's two wives, Ahinoam the Jezreelitess, and Abigail the widow of Nabal the Carmelite, had been taken captive.

6 Now David was greatly distressed, for the people spoke of stoning him, because the soul of all the people was grieved, every man for his sons and his daughters. But David strengthened himself in the Lord his God."

8 And David enquired at the LORD, saying, Shall I pursue after this troop? shall I overtake them? And he answered him, Pursue: for thou shalt surely overtake them, and without fail recover all." 1st Samuel 30: 1-6; 8 (NKJV)

It is normal to feel the pressure that comes from the oppression of the enemy. However, we can proof of our maturity in God in the way we handle these difficult situations.

For David, the first step was to encourage or strengthen himself in the Lord. Every child of God should do likewise because He is the source of our strength. Besides, one thing that we should never do is run after the enemy without due consideration of all possibilities. We should not allow our enemy to dictate our battle plan.

As his second step, David consulted the Lord for his course of action. Perhaps because he knows that the way of man is not in himself because it is not in man to direct his steps. For the Lord orders the steps of a good man and delights in his way.

Thirdly, He pursued the enemy and recovered all because that was the will of God concerning him in that instant. We have to be in tune with God's will for us at every step of our walk with Him. We should ask him to lead us in his truth as he teaches us his way. His answer is not always affirmative. Sometimes He can say, "Wait until …" In that case,

"Wait on the Lord: be of good courage, and he shall strengthen thine heart: wait, I say, on the Lord."
Psalm 27:14

"Rest in the LORD, and wait patiently for him: fret not thyself because of him who prospereth in his way, because of the man who bringeth wicked devices to pass."
Psalms 37:7

The impact of the Vietnam War in the United States is worth noting. Its effect was similar to that of the Nigerian civil war. It was an era filled with increased acts of disobedience in the forms of protest against the war. Morale was low and many young people fled the country to avoid the

The Battle in Progress

draft into the armed forces. Frustration and a sense of hopelessness triggered riots in some cities.

It does not matter whether the war is external or internal; the effect of the devastation is the same. The same can be true of spiritual warfare, if you are not on the winning side. It does not matter much where it starts; its aim is always to shake our faith in God and to separate us from Him. Nevertheless,

"8 We are hard pressed on every side, but not crushed; perplexed, but not in despair;

9 persecuted, but not abandoned; struck down, but not destroyed

10 We always carry around in our body the death of Jesus, so that the life of Jesus may also be revealed in our body"
2nd *Corinthians 4:8-10 (NIV)*

Yes, we feel the pain, the persecution and the humiliation that accompany living a Godly life but with each battle, we grow stronger in Him as we learn to walk with Him.

"7 For God hath not given us the spirit of fear; but of power, and of love, and of a sound mind.

8 Be not thou therefore ashamed of the testimony of our Lord, nor of me his prisoner: but be thou partaker of the afflictions of the gospel according to the power of God;

9 Who hath saved us, and called us with an holy calling, not according to our works, but according to his own purpose and grace, which was given us in Christ Jesus before the world began," 2nd *Timothy 1:7-9*

"12 For the which cause I also suffer these things: nevertheless I am not ashamed: for I know whom I have believed, and am persuaded that he is able to keep that which I have committed unto him against that day."

2nd *Timothy 1:12*

To those of us therefore who believe, whom God has called, sanctified and preserved in Jesus Christ, Jude the brother of Our Lord Jesus Christ wrote:

"3 Beloved, when I gave all diligence to write unto you of the common salvation, it was needful for me to write unto you, and exhort you that ye should earnestly contend for the faith which was once delivered unto the saints." Jude 1:3

He wrote to give us some insight into the spiritual battle in progress and to encourage us as we walk with God. I can hear him say, "I wanted to write to you to tell about the privileges that God has given us, to be born again of water and of the Spirit. I wanted you to know that God has separated us unto Himself for every good work. I wanted to share with you the wonderful experience of being in Him, not having the righteousness, which is rooted in legality, but rather the imputed righteousness of God, which is by the faith of Jesus Christ unto all and upon all those that believe. I did not know what great a gift God had given to me when He gave me Jesus Christ for an older brother. I wish I knew. Now that I know, He is closer to me than ever before. I wanted to write to you about the common salvation that we share but I would rather first write to you about your faith."

It is as though he sees in this generation, believers who are loitering aimlessly in the battlefield. Therefore, he writes to tell us about the thing that is needful, being our faith, and to exhort us that we should earnestly fight to maintain and continue in that faith, because it is the faith of Our Lord Jesus Christ, which at one time, He handed over to the saints. God did not call us to a continuous cycle of victory and defeat. Rather He called us to a productive life; to bear fruits that would remain, to maintain and use the measure of the faith

The Battle in Progress

that He has given us today as a stepping-stone on which we stand as we peek into our future in Him, a future that is full of great promises and victories.

You see while the giant was asleep, certain things happened in the church and led to the abuse of the grace of God as well as to the denying of the only Lord God and our Lord Jesus Christ.

> *"4 For there are certain men crept in unawares, who were before of old ordained to this condemnation, ungodly men, turning the grace of our God into lasciviousness, and denying the only Lord God, and our Lord Jesus Christ."*
>
> *Jude 1: 4*

Jesus said:

> *"But know this, that if the goodman of the house had known in what watch the thief would come, he would have watched, and would not have suffered his house to be **broken up**." Matthew 24:43*

> *"And this know, that if the goodman of the house had known what hour the thief would come, he would have watched, and not have suffered his house to be **broken through**." Luke 12:39.*

Sometimes, the devil comes to pitch his tent in our lives, homes and businesses. At other times, he just wants to blow through like a hurricane leaving behind trails of broken hearts and homes. Sometimes, after he starts the confusion and every work of darkness against

> **God has called us to a productive life; to bear fruits that would remain, to maintain and use the measure of the faith that He has given us today as a stepping-stone on which we stand as we peek into our future in Him, a future that is full of great promises and victories.**

us, he would leave for a season only to come back later on. Be certain that he will return to check on his prey and to make sure that it remains bound in his snare. This is the approach that I call "breaking through" by the devil. However, when he does come to break up, he would not leave after his havoc, but rather he would stay on to insure that his prey remains trapped. Jesus explains:

"24 When the unclean spirit is gone out of a man, he walketh through dry places, seeking rest; and finding none, he saith, I will return unto my house whence I came out .

25 And when he cometh, he findeth it swept and garnished.

26 Then goeth he, and taketh to him seven other spirits more wicked than himself; and they enter in, and dwell there: and the last state of that man is worse than the first."
Luke 11:24-26

My brethren, we are involved in a war with an all-encompassing battlefield. This war is not in the natural realm, though it affects us naturally. Ours is a spiritual fight against spiritual beings operating in the spiritual realms. Therefore:

"Be sober, be vigilant; because your adversary the devil, as a roaring lion, walketh about, seeking whom he may devour:" 1st Peter 5:8

This is not a new war, neither are the enemies new, they have always been there. After you and I are gone to glory, they will look for other Saints to fight. These are enemies "who were before of old ordained to this condemnation."

They were ordained to fight the church. It does not matter what we do, they will always come after us. Therefore, there is no need for us to think that we will reach that place in God, while still here on earth, where we will no longer have to fight. There is no need for us to think that we will reach that

The Battle in Progress

place in Christ that the devil will stop seeking to destroy us. He will always seek to destroy us. He is always seeking to steal, to kill and to destroy. However, Jesus said:

> *"... I am come that they might have life, and that they might have it more abundantly". John 10:10*

Let us not forget that God has given us dominion over all the earth and the power to subdue every thing that creeps upon the surface of the earth. For of the first Adam:

> *"¶ ... God said, Let us make man in our image, after our likeness: and let them have dominion over the fish of the sea, and over the fowl of the air, and over the cattle, and over all the earth, and over every creeping thing that creepeth upon the earth." Genesis 1:26*

Of the second Adam:

> *"9 ... God also hath highly exalted him, and given him a name which is above every name:*
>
> *10 That at the name of Jesus every knee should bow, of things in heaven, and things in earth, and things under the earth;*
>
> *11 And that every tongue should confess that Jesus Christ is Lord, to the glory of God the Father." Philippians 2:9-11*

> *"Wherefore he saith, When he ascended up on high, he led captivity captive, and gave gifts unto men." Ephesians 4:8*

To the Church, Jesus said:

> *"Behold, I give unto you power to tread on serpents and scorpions, and over all the power of the enemy: and nothing shall by any means hurt you." Luke 10:19*

Yes, we have an enemy who desires to sift us as wheat. We know that our adversary is going back and forth in the earth and walking up and down in it looking for victims.

However, as the elect of GOD, fight the good fight of faith, take hold of the eternal life to which he called you and for which he made the good confession in the presence of many witnesses. For if God be for us, who can be against us?

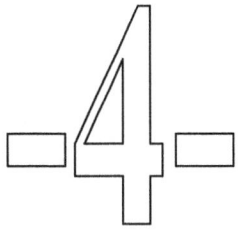

THE ARENA OF SPIRITUAL WARFARE

We have already discussed the fact that spiritual warfare is ongoing and takes place all around us. Now we will focus on the arena of the warfare. You see whenever there is a war between two groups or entities, a sound and strategic approach calls for selective targeting of the enemy. The plan is usually to deliver a swift and overpowering strike to targets that would quickly weaken the enemy and take away its will to fight. To accomplish this, one must know the strengths and weaknesses of the enemy. In addition, the targets selected carefully, must include the enemy's areas of strength and vital interest.

This is also the case in spiritual warfare. Our enemy knows that many of us have chosen to serve God. He knows that for some of us, to live is Christ and to die is gain. In addition, that:

"Ye are of God, little children, and have overcome them: because greater is he that is in you, than he that is in the world." 1John 4:4

For these and other good reasons, in selecting his targets, he goes for those, which if compromised, will most likely disconnect us from God. Our adversary realizes that all power in heaven and in earth belongs to Jesus Christ, and that it impossible for him to win any scrimmage against Christ. Therefore, he goes looking for other targets to kill and destroy.

THE BODY OF CHRIST

The main target of the enemy is the body of Christ, which is the church as it is written:

> *"9 And the great dragon was cast out, that old serpent, called the Devil, and Satan, which deceiveth the whole world: he was cast out into the earth, and his angels were cast out with him.*
> *10 And I heard a loud voice saying in heaven, Now is come salvation, and strength, and the kingdom of our God, and the power of his Christ: for the accuser of our brethren is cast down, which accused them before our God day and night.*
> *17 And the dragon was wroth with the woman, and went to make war with the remnant of her seed, which keep the commandments of God, and have the testimony of Jesus Christ." Revelation 12:9-10; 17*

It is not easy to live a Godly life. As soon as we choose Christ, and become added to the Church, the devil automatically adds us to the list of defectors from his camp. As such, he comes after us because we have become members of the Body of Christ. We know that the devil will go wherever the children of God gather, with accusations and lies, working through the children of disobedience. At one point, when speaking to the world, Jesus said:

> *"Ye are of your father the devil, and the lusts of your father ye will do. He was a murderer from the beginning, and abode not in the truth, because there is no truth in him.*

The Arena of Spiritual Warfare

When he speaketh a lie, he speaketh of his own: for he is a liar, and the father of it." John 8:44

It is important for us to recognize these workers of iniquity; for though we do not fight against natural beings, they are the ones most often used of the devil to afflict us. Our Lord exhorts us to recognize the fact that:

"18 If the world hate you, ye know that it hated me before it hated you.
19 If ye were of the world, the world would love his own: but because ye are not of the world, but I have chosen you out of the world, therefore the world hateth you."
John 15:18-19

Nevertheless, the scripture asks:

"35 Who shall separate us from the love of Christ? shall tribulation, or distress, or persecution, or famine, or nakedness, or peril, or sword?
36 As it is written, For thy sake we are killed all the day long; we are accounted as sheep for the slaughter.
37 Nay, in all these things we are more than conquerors through him that loved us." Romans 8:35-37

Yes, the devil does come to fight against the remnant in the Church. But, Apostle Peter writes to encourage us. He says:

"12 ¶ Beloved, think it not strange concerning the fiery trial which is to try you, as though some strange thing happened unto you:
13 But rejoice, inasmuch as ye are partakers of Christ's sufferings; that, when his glory shall be revealed, ye may be glad also with exceeding joy." 1st Peter 4:12-13

Our rejoicing is not only in tribulation, it is even more so in the knowledge of the fact that Satan is already a defeated foe. As members of the body of Christ, we must remember, that God has indeed purchased us with the blood of Jesus

Christ. Therefore, our victory lies in our ability to look up to our Redeemer while we stand ready to testify always of His sustaining power that is at work in us even during the testing of our faith.

> *"4 For whatsoever is born of God overcometh the world: and this is the victory that overcometh the world, even our faith.*
> *5 Who is he that overcometh the world, but he that believeth that Jesus is the Son of God?" 1John 5:4, 5*

Since God has armed us with the blood of the Lamb and given us the testimony, that He is able to do exceeding and abundantly above all that, we could ever ask or think:

> *"Submit yourselves therefore to God. Resist the devil, and he will flee from you." James 4:7*
> *"Be sober, be vigilant; because your adversary the devil, as a roaring lion, walketh about, seeking whom he may devour:" 1st Peter 5:8*

THE MIND OF THE BELIEVER

The mind of the child of God is another favorite target of the enemy. You see the mind is distinctly our reflective consciousness. Some say that it is "the organ of moral thinking and knowing" or rather put differently, "the intellectual organ of moral sentiment". God hath not given us the spirit of fear; but of power, and of love, and of a sound mind.

In our minds reside the aptitude of understanding and those of judging, as with our thoughts, feelings, purposes, and desires. It is with our minds that we perceive divine things, recognize goodness and hate evil. Paul writes:

> *"21 I find then a law, that, when I would do good, evil is present with me.*
> *22 For I delight in the law of God after the inward man:*

The Arena of Spiritual Warfare

23 But I see another law in my members, warring against the law of my mind, and bringing me into captivity to the law of sin which is in my members." Romans 7:21-23

The devil knows that if he can pollute our minds with all that is in the world, he can diminish our ability to receive, understand and operate according to God's spiritual truth. We see here in Paul, a desire to serve God in Spirit and in truth. We also see that desire under a constant challenge by the activities of his mind as long as he lived in his mortal body. Therefore, he cried:

"24 O wretched man that I am! who shall deliver me from the body of this death?
25 I thank God through Jesus Christ our Lord. So then with the mind I myself serve the law of God; but with the flesh the law of sin." Romans 7:24-25

The battle over our mind is not new strategy. The devil does desire to sift us as wheat. For since the beginning of time, the truth has been that to access the true and perfect will of God, there must be a transformation of the mind. Yet somehow, many children of God have allowed their mind to sway with every wind of doctrine, deceit and cunningly devised fable with which, the devil attacks our minds. Howbeit, the word of God encourages us to set our affection on things above, not on things on the earth.

Most internal struggles are results of indecisions. When we cannot make up our mind, we allow fear and doubt to paralyze us and to turn our focus from God.

We know that if we draw close to God, He will draw close to us. However, if we remain double minded and faithless the truth also remains:

"7 For let not that man think that he shall receive any thing of the Lord.
8 A double minded man is unstable in all his ways."
James 1:7-8

When you have trouble on every side, when there are squabbles and stressful conditions all around you, when you are dealing with emotional turmoil and fears in your mind, remember: God will keep in perfect peace, those who focus their mind on Him, because they trust in Him.

If you can only trust in God and learn to depend on Him, you will surely come to know that:

"7 Blessed is the man that trusteth in the LORD, and whose hope the LORD is.
8 For he shall be as a tree planted by the waters, and that spreadeth out her roots by the river, and shall not see when heat cometh, but her leaf shall be green; and shall not be careful in the year of drought, neither shall cease from yielding fruit." Jeremiah 17:7-8

You have probably heard people say, "I think I am loosing my mind". That may not be too far from the truth, for there is a thief on the loose. Let us not give place to him but rather, be renewed in the spirit of our mind. For to us it is written:

"Wherefore gird up the loins of your mind, be sober, and hope to the end for the grace that is to be brought unto you at the revelation of Jesus Christ;" 1st Peter 1:13

THE BODY OF THE BELIEVER

Another strategic target of the enemy is our body, which for the purpose of this discussion comprises our health, sense of well-being and quality of life. These are usually under the attack of the enemy because he believes that if he weakens our body through much affliction and turn our whole world upside down, he may gain access to our mind. With this in mind, it becomes obvious that our bodily travails are nothing but cunningly devised means of the devil to get us to reject God in our minds or to curse Him and die. Let us listen in on this conversation between God and the devil concerning Job.

The Arena of Spiritual Warfare

> *"3 And the LORD said unto Satan, Hast thou considered my servant Job, that there is none like him in the earth, a perfect and an upright man, one that feareth God, and escheweth evil? and still he holdeth fast his integrity, although thou movedst me against him, to destroy him without cause.*
> *4 And Satan answered the LORD, and said, Skin for skin, yea, all that a man hath will he give for his life.*
> *5 But put forth thine hand now, and touch his bone and his flesh, and he will curse thee to thy face." Job 2:3-5*

The devil some how believes that our desire for self-preservation exceeds our need to be found faithful unto God. He believes that a right combination of pain and suffering in your natural body will cause us to wonder if God is really with us. Our adversary knows that questioning whether God has thoughts of good concerning us during our times of trial, will generally open a door of conversation with him and lead us into his trap. If he touched your bone and your flesh, what would you do?

We should not be surprised at the ever-increasing number of diseases in our days. It seems as though every time man discovers a cure for one disease, a few more diseases would spring up. Could this be the work of an enemy? Of course, yes. If so, what then do we do? Well let us follow the example of Paul in his handling of the messenger of Satan sent to buffet him. Of this, he writes:

> *"7 And lest I should be exalted above measure through the abundance of the revelations, there was given to me a thorn in the flesh, the messenger of Satan to buffet me, lest I should be exalted above measure.*
> *8 For this thing I besought the Lord thrice, that it might depart from me.*

9 And he said unto me, My grace is sufficient for thee: for my strength is made perfect in weakness."
2nd Corinthians 12:7-9a

Of course, the messenger from hell will come asking us to submit ourselves to him for a temporary reprieve from our current situation or circumstance. However, our position should be such that we give no place to him. Rather no matter what the situation may be, we should always seek Jesus Christ and His will concerning our lives. Moreover, although it is okay to express our desire, we should always yield to his will. Remember to always and:

"In every thing give thanks: for this is the will of God in Christ Jesus concerning you." 1Thessalonians 5:18

We need to realize that we are not alone when our body is under the attack of the enemy, for He who is faithful has said, "I will never leave you nor forsake you." Paul said:

"9 ... Most gladly therefore will I rather glory in my infirmities, that the power of Christ may rest upon me.
10 Therefore I take pleasure in infirmities, in reproaches, in necessities, in persecutions, in distresses for Christ's sake: for when I am weak, then am I strong."
2nd Corinthians 12:9b-10

Paul understood that his afflictions and sufferings were part of the will of God concerning him so he gladly yielded to them. Having thus yielded, he waited for the revelation of God's glory in his situations, knowing that they would all work out for his good. He did not stop what he was doing to wait for that revelation, but rather while he was waiting; he elevated his pursuit of Christ to the extent that he said:

"10 That I may know him, and the power of his resurrection, and the fellowship of his sufferings, being made conformable unto his death;" Philippians 3:10

The Arena of Spiritual Warfare

Many times, we focus so much on our afflictions that we lose sight of the big picture. That Christ suffered for us. Can you imagine how he looked after forty days and night of consecration, of fasting, and of being tempted for our sake? He was probably not much different from the sick, the poor, and the homeless that we have among us today, who the society in general does overlook, without respect, and over whom many assume air of superiority. Yet it was through much self-sacrifice that Christ proved his own obedience. For when He took on the form of a man, he humbled himself so that he can be an example for us to learn that our troubles will not last forever. What is more, in place of these trials, will be the manifestation of the power of the Holy Spirit working in our lives.

> *"13 And when the devil had ended all the temptation, he departed from him for a season.*
> *14 ¶ And Jesus returned in the power of the Spirit into Galilee: and there went out a fame of him through all the region round about." Luke 4:13-14*

Let us make up our minds to seek our Lord in whatever state we may find ourselves.

> *"1 ¶ Forasmuch then as Christ hath suffered for us in the flesh, arm yourselves likewise with the same mind: for he that hath suffered in the flesh hath ceased from sin;*
>
> *2 That he no longer should live the rest of his time in the flesh to the lusts of men, but to the will of God."*
> 1st *Peter 4:1-2*

Is it always the will of God for us to subject to sicknesses and bear bodily afflictions or diseases? God forbid. For it is written:

> *"Beloved, I wish above all things that thou mayest prosper and be in health, even as thy soul prospereth." 3rd John 1:2*

Moreover, we know that with every stripe that He took on our behalf, He purchased our healing, not just for our souls but for our bodies also. That is why David said:

> *"2 Bless the LORD, O my soul, and forget not all his benefits:*
> *3 Who forgiveth all thine iniquities; who healeth all thy diseases;" Psalms 103:2-3*

He gave to them that believe power to lay hands on the sick that they may recover. He also gave to the church, the gifts of healing through the Holy Spirit. Therefore, it is said:

> *"14 Is any sick among you? let him call for the elders of the church; and let them pray over him, anointing him with oil in the name of the Lord:*
> *15 And the prayer of faith shall save the sick, and the Lord shall raise him up; and if he have committed sins, they shall be forgiven him." James 5:14-15*

Yes the devil may target our body but he has no rights to it except as permitted by God. He, Satan knows that the LORD has made a hedge about us, and about our homes, and about all that we have on every side. That God has blessed the work of our hands, as well as all that he has given us. Therefore, if the devil should attack you without proper permission, God has put in the Church all that is necessary to bring him to subjection. On the other hand, if it is God's will that you be afflicted:

> *"... fear not them which kill the body, but are not able to kill the soul: but rather fear him which is able to destroy both soul and body in hell." Matthew 10:28*

> *"But rejoice, inasmuch as ye are partakers of Christ's sufferings; that, when his glory shall be revealed, ye may be glad also with exceeding joy." 1st Peter 4:13*

THE SOUL OF THE BELIEVER

Yet another prime target of the enemy is the soul of the believer. Understanding God's position concerning the Soul is that:

"The soul that sinneth, it shall die. The son shall not bear the iniquity of the father, neither shall the father bear the iniquity of the son: the righteousness of the righteous shall be upon him, and the wickedness of the wicked shall be upon him." Ezekiel 18:20

The devil has purposed therefore to subvert the souls of men by turning them from the truth, which is in Christ Jesus. The question may be asked, what exactly is the human Soul? Well, the soul of man is a living being. It is our immortal part, which at the end of our mortal life, continues to have a permanent individual existence. This existence can only be in one of two places, heaven or hell depending on the relationship that we have with God.

"5 ...For there is going to come a day of judgment when God, the just judge of all the world,
6 will judge all people according to what they have done.
7 He will give eternal life to those who persist in doing what is good, seeking after the glory and honor and immortality that God offers.
8 But he will pour out his anger and wrath on those who live for themselves, who refuse to obey the truth and practice evil deeds.
9 There will be trouble and calamity for everyone who keeps on sinning – for the Jew first and also for the Gentile.
10 But there will be glory and honor and peace from God for all who do good – for the Jew first and also for the Gentile.
11 For God does not show favoritism."

Romans 2:5b-11(NLT)

The devil realizes that our soul is the seat of our feelings, desires, likes, and dislikes. For this reason, he focuses his attack on it through the manipulation of our senses. He uses the spirit of lusts and the spirit of pride to seduce our souls. We know these lusts to be the lust of the flesh, the lust of the eyes, and the pride to be the pride of life. Since we cannot see our souls, often times we lose touch with it and its needs. We do not realize or discern that our soul is fighting for its survival. Nonetheless, the battle continues and we are cautioned:

"Dearly beloved, I beseech you as strangers and pilgrims, abstain from fleshly lusts, which war against the soul;"
1st Peter 2:11

The greatest danger that our soul faces is neglect. Unfortunately, we do not have the devil to blame for this, since the cause is not directly from him. This neglect is self-inflicted. Yes, the devil does plant the seed that sets the wheel in motion, but we have the power of choice. We can choose to gain the world and loose our soul or primarily pursue God, His kingdom and righteousness and gain the world by virtue of our position as heirs of God and joint-heirs with Christ.

"39 But we are not of them who draw back unto perdition; but of them that believe to the saving of the soul."
Hebrews 10: 39

Brethren, it behooves us to fight for our soul. My prayer is
"that He would grant you, according to the riches of His glory, to be strengthened with power through His Spirit in the inner man," Ephesians 3:16

"And the very God of peace sanctify you wholly; and I pray God your whole spirit and soul and body be preserved blameless unto the coming of our Lord Jesus Christ."
1st Thessalonians 5:23

The Arena of Spiritual Warfare

OUR PURPOSE – THE REASON FOR YOUR EXISTENCE

We must realize that our God given purpose in life is one of our adversary's constant targets. Merriam-Webster defines purpose as "something set up as an object or an end to be attained." It is the object toward which one strives, or for which something exists. According to some philosophies, purpose is central to a good human life. Helen Keller, who altered our perception of the disabled and remapped the boundaries of sight and sense, wrote that happiness comes from "fidelity to a worthy purpose"

In the bible, God tells us that His thoughts for us are thoughts of peace aimed at leading us to an expected end. The thought of God toward us, His children, is His purpose for us. It is for this reason that He gives us His Spirit to guide us to that expected end. When we embrace His purpose for us, it becomes the object that we reach for or the main goal that we must accomplish. It also becomes our point of focus or aim to which we direct our view.

So you see the problem that the devil has, is not with the fact that God has a purpose for us, but rather that we strive to pursue our purpose. Satan desires to come against everything in our lives that enables us to be in unity with God and His purpose for us. He knows that as we remain obedient to God, trusting and dependent on God through the finished work of Jesus Christ, changes will occur in our lives through the leading of the Spirit of Christ. These changes will enable us and lead us to attaining our purpose as everything that is unlike Him, give way to His divine will and purpose for us. For:

"¶ The LORD of hosts hath sworn, saying, Surely as I have thought, so shall it come to pass; and as I have purposed, so shall it stand:" Isaiah 14: 24

THE ACCESS TO OUR DESTINY

For every purpose, there is a place, a time and a provision. Each one of us has a set place in God where our purpose resides. That place is our divine destination or destiny. It is for reaching that destination that we should strive, and for carrying out our purpose in our destiny that we should live. Notice that even the salmons understand this concept. They understand that their primary purpose is to bring in the next generation. For this, they are not only willing to swim up stream, but also go through a process of adaptation to freshwater before heading upstream to spawn. God said to Jeremiah,

> *"Before I formed thee in the belly I knew thee; and before thou camest forth out of the womb I sanctified thee, and I ordained thee a prophet unto the nations." Jeremiah 1:5*

For Jeremiah, his expected end was to be a prophet to the Nations. God orders the steps of those who trust in Him to get them to the place where they will flow in the anointing for which He called them. When God called Abraham, He told him to go to the land that he will show him. Today, many of us have heard a call from God. It is a call that takes us from our place of comfort and exposes us to the uncharted territories in our lives. It is during this journey to our destiny with God, that we find ourselves under attack by the enemy.

Therefore, as you press toward God's plan for you, expect some opposition because Satan's plan is to hinder, frustrate, distract and ultimately prevent you from reaching your divine destiny. These attacks are because we are striving to get to our place and position in God. If you do not become weary but press on to the end, you will hear your Master say *"Well done, thou good and faithful servant"* and for me, that is worth it all.

The Arena of Spiritual Warfare

THE SEASON OF GOD'S FAVOR (OUR SET TIME)

One of the most vulnerable times in the life of the child of God is the time between the revelation of their purpose and the attainment of that purpose. We spend this period typically on the potter's wheel as God molds us and prepares us for the role ahead.

> *"13 And the LORD said unto Abraham, Wherefore did Sarah laugh, saying, Shall I of a surety bear a child, which am old?" Genesis 18:13*

During this time, the devil magnifies all our inadequacies as faith gives way to anxiety, weariness and uncertainty. Do not allow Satan to trick you. Wait for the appointed time.

> *"14 Is any thing too hard for the LORD? At the time appointed I will return unto thee, according to the time of life, and Sarah shall have a son." Genesis 18:14*

Nothing is too hard for God. Do not allow the enemy to steal your seed from you? You see God does not make promises that He cannot bring to pass. We have to understand that God's plan may not always unfold right away. However, slowly, steadily, surely, the time approaches when the vision will be fulfilled. If it seems slow, wait patiently, for it will surely take place. There is a set time for every promise and purpose.

> *"2 For Sarah conceived, and bare Abraham a son in his old age, at the set time of which God had spoken to him."*
> *Genesis 21:2*

With this in mind, we must fight against every form of discouragement remembering that hope deferred makes the heart sick, but when the desire comes, it is a tree of life. We must hope continually in God and praise Him the more while we wait.

> *"Wait on the LORD: be of good courage, and he shall strengthen thine heart: wait, I say, on the LORD"*
> *Psalms 27:14*

When the children of Israel left Egypt, they were a collection of families but they arrived in Canaan as a nation. Through forty years of humiliation and testing, God transformed them making them His people and teaching them to trust and depend only on Him. Moses speaking to them in the wilderness said:

> *" Be careful to obey all the commands I am giving you today. Then you will live and multiply, and you will enter and occupy the land the LORD swore to give your ancestors.*
> *2 Remember how the LORD your God led you through the wilderness for forty years, humbling you and testing you to prove your character, and to find out whether or not you would really obey his commands.*
> *3 Yes, he humbled you by letting you go hungry and then feeding you with manna, a food previously unknown to you and your ancestors. He did it to teach you that people need more than bread for their life; real life comes by feeding on every word of the LORD." Deuteronomy 8:1-3 (NLT)*

We have to be mindful of our character and our behaviors lest we also displease God as we transition to our destiny.

> *"But with many of them God was not well pleased: for they were overthrown in the wilderness" 1st Corinthians 10:5*

Do not let the devil plant seeds of disobedience, discontent and murmuring in your spirit thereby causing you to "bite the very hand that feeds you" and consequently fall from the grace and will of God for you.

The Arena of Spiritual Warfare

GOD'S PROVISION

For every purpose, there is a place, a time and provision. God has given us, His children, tremendous provisions through his numerous promises, and the devil knows that. Unfortunately, however many of us do not know the time of God's visitation, neither do we know the provisions He has made available to work together for our good. Yet, because we belong to Christ, he has blessed us with every spiritual blessing in the heavenly realms. He beckons us to call on him so that He can show us great and mighty things that we have in Him.

"In whom also we have obtained an inheritance, being predestinated according to the purpose of him who worketh all things after the counsel of his own will:" Ephesians 1:11

We have natural as well as spiritual inheritance in Christ. The inheritances are His provision for us; these gifts are great targets of contention by the devil. Of the spiritual gifts to the church, it is written,

"11 And he gave some, apostles; and some, prophets; and some, evangelists; and some, pastors and teachers;
12 For the perfecting of the saints, for the work of the ministry, for the edifying of the body of Christ:
13 Till we all come in the unity of the faith, and of the knowledge of the Son of God, unto a perfect man, unto the measure of the stature of the fulness of Christ:
14 That we henceforth be no more children, tossed to and fro, and carried about with every wind of doctrine, by the sleight of men, and cunning craftiness, whereby they lie in wait to deceive;
15 But speaking the truth in love, may grow up into him in all things, which is the head, even Christ:
16 From whom the whole body fitly joined together and compacted by that which every joint supplieth, according

to the effectual working in the measure of every part, maketh increase of the body unto the edifying of itself in love." Ephesians 4:12-16

These gifts should be used for the building and uniting of the body of Christ, through LOVE. Instead, we have allowed the enemy to use denominational and doctrinal differences as well as strive and contention to rob the church of God's precious gifts.

Likewise, concerning spiritual gifts (the word of wisdom; the word of knowledge; faith; the gifts of healing; the working of miracles; prophecy; discerning of spirits; divers kinds of tongues; the interpretation of tongues) the bible teaches:

"4 Now there are diversities of gifts, but the same Spirit.
5 And there are differences of administrations, but the same Lord.
6 And there are diversities of operations, but it is the same God which worketh all in all.
7 But the manifestation of the Spirit is given to every man to profit withal." Ephesians 4:4-7

Yet perhaps because of lack of knowledge or the fear of losing control of the people, many assemblies have suppressed the free flow of these gifts of which God wants shared with all. Do not be dismayed because the devil is attacking us on every front. He attacks our homes and relationships, seeking to destroy them, as he does so many other gifts in the church today. It is a shame to say that there is almost no difference between the divorce rate in the world and that among believers. Furthermore, it is common today, to find husbands leaving their wives for other men and wives leaving their husbands for other women. This is nothing but the attack of the devil.

The Arena of Spiritual Warfare

You may also notice that our children are facing greater exposure to cunningly devised tools of the devil designed to entice and draw them away from the very foundation on which they stand. Some of us, who should know better, are cutting our noses off to spite our faces by falling out with the God of our salvation. But,

"Thus saith the LORD, thy Redeemer, the Holy One of Israel; I am the LORD thy God which teacheth thee to profit, which leadeth thee by the way that thou shouldest go." Isaiah 48:17

Now concerning material wealth, God's wish is that we would prosper. He is the one who gives us the increase. He sets us up so that we should be the head and not the tail. For the children of Israel, He supplied manna, quails and water in their hour of need. To Elijah, God sent the ravens to supply his need as he waited in the brook that He had sent him. We also know that God continued to take care of him using widow whom He had prepared. Jesus Christ is the same even today. He has promised never to leave us. Paul also tells us that God shall supply all our need according to his riches in glory by Christ Jesus. He continues:

"11 Not that I speak in respect of want: for I have learned, in whatsoever state I am, therewith to be content.
12 I know both how to be abased, and I know how to abound: every where and in all things I am instructed both to be full and to be hungry, both to abound and to suffer need.
13 I can do all things through Christ which strengtheneth me." Philippians 4:11-13

When we become rooted in Christ, the spirit of lack cannot separate us from God or cause us to be distracted from the truth.

Often times, when God has blessed us, the devil tries to use a proud spirit to trick us to think that our achievements are because of our own strength and natural abilities. Therefore, keep in mind that pride goes before destruction and a haughty spirit before a fall, for a man's pride shall bring him low: but honor shall uphold the humble in spirit. And:

"18 .... remember the LORD thy God: for it is he that giveth thee power to get wealth, that he may establish his covenant which he sware unto thy fathers, as it is this day. 19 And it shall be, if thou do at all forget the LORD thy God, and walk after other gods, and serve them, and worship them, I testify against you this day that ye shall surely perish." Deuteronomy 8:18-19

In conclusion, we have looked at some of the devils targets in spiritual warfare. We have noticed that in choosing these targets, the devil desires to deter us from running to the end, the race that is set before us. Over the centuries and through many generations, his targets have not changed; neither should our confident in God. Like David, let us seek after God's heart, trusting that:

"2 When the wicked, even mine enemies and my foes, came upon me to eat up my flesh, they stumbled and fell.

3 Though an host should encamp against me, my heart shall not fear: though war should rise against me, in this will I be confident.

5 For in the time of trouble he shall hide me in his pavilion: in the secret of his tabernacle shall he hide me; he shall set me up upon a rock.

6 And now shall mine head be lifted up above mine enemies round about me: therefore will I offer in his tabernacle sacrifices of joy; I will sing, yea, I will sing praises unto the LORD." Psalms 27:2-3, 5-6

THE ENEMY OF THE SAINTS

I stated earlier, that whereas some enlist to fight the good fight of faith, others are drafted and the rest, caught loitering aimlessly in the battlefield. The truth is, no matter how you got involved, you must become committed to the cause or find yourself in the state of a deserter. The bible tells us of the multitude that followed Christ; it also tells us that when they wanted to become His disciples, He admonished them to make sure that they were willing to the pay price that that would be require of them as His disciples. This is not to say, that Jesus did not want the multitude to follow Him, but that they should have their mind made up because no man, having put his hand to the plough, and looking back, is fit for the kingdom of God.

We are a chosen generation, a royal priesthood, a holy nation, God's own special people, called out of darkness into His marvelous light to proclaim His praises. He has sent us to open the eyes of those who are blind to the light of the gospel, to turn them from darkness to light and from the power of Satan unto God, so that they may receive forgiveness of sins, and inheritance among those sanctified by faith in Him. For these reasons, he wants us grounded in Him and connected to

Him. He also wants us to know the enemy we will encounter as we walk with Him. For Jesus said:

> *"31 Or what king, going to make war against another king, sitteth not down first, and consulteth whether he be able with ten thousand to meet him that cometh against him with twenty thousand?*
> *32 Or else, while the other is yet a great way off, he sendeth an ambassage, and desireth conditions of peace."*
> Luke 14:31-32 (KJV)

We do not use the same method to fight all enemies or resolve all conflicts. While some enemies, or conflicts can be subdued through prayer only, fasting as well as prayer is required if we desire to prevail against spiritual strongholds. God has given the gift of discernment of spirits to the church because it is imperative that we know our enemy. We need to sense him coming while he is yet a great way off, so that we can prepare ourselves and stand in guard against him. To be victorious in our fight, we need more than a casual awareness of our enemy's existence. We need to know his organization, targets, strategies and weapons. We need to know, not feel. Be aware that emotionalism or zeal will not take you far enough. Only strategic and deliberate decisions followed by actions born out of obedience and total submission to God's will, will take you to your victorious end. For,

> **Be aware that emotionalism or zeal will not take you far enough. Only strategic and deliberate decisions followed by actions born out of obedience and submission to God's will, will take you to your victorious end.**

> *"A wise man scaleth the city of the mighty, and casteth down the strength of the confidence thereof."*
> *Proverbs 21:22 (KJV)*

The Enemy of The Saints

The bible tells us that we do not fight flesh and blood. We are fighting against an enemy whose power is very great in the world. This 'city of the mighty' thinks very highly of itself seeing that he is the prince of this world, but we must destroy his vain reasoning and arguments. We must dismantle every high thing on which he relies as he exalts itself against the knowledge of God. We must subdue every divisive thought of his and bring it into captivity to the obedience of Christ. We should not go hastily into battle against this enemy but, first we must sit consult with our God who is omnipotent, omniscient and omnipresent, who sees the weapon even as it is formed against us and even before its formation. Our God is the discerner of secrets, even the secret thoughts of men. Therefore, wisdom requires that we wait for the leading of His Spirit, who establishes our purpose through his counsel:

> **While some enemies, or conflicts can be subdued through prayer only, fasting as well as prayer is required if we desire to prevail against spiritual strongholds.**

> *"For by wise counsel thou shalt make thy war: and in multitude of counsellors there is safety." Proverbs 24:6*

THE OBJECTIVES OF YOUR ENEMY

Christ clearly outlined the objective of the devil, our enemy who he also calls a thief. He said that:

> *'The thief cometh not, but for to steal, and to kill, and to destroy: I am come that they might have life, and that they might have it more abundantly.' John 10:10*

A thief is one who steals especially sneakily or secretly. He is one who commits theft or breaking and entering, a criminal who takes someone else's property with the intention of keeping it. On the other hand, if the legal owner of a property grants permission to another, to take and keep their property, that person to whom permission is granted is not a thief.

The point here is that the child of God must be careful to ensure that the thief initiates every attack without our permission. We have to make sure that we do not leave the door cracked for things to creep in. For if, we create an environment conducive for the devil, he will come together with his friends and dwell therein.

> *"7 Be not deceived; God is not mocked: for whatsoever a man soweth, that shall he also reap.*
> *8 For he that soweth to his flesh shall of the flesh reap corruption; but he that soweth to the Spirit shall of the Spirit reap life everlasting." Galatians 6:7-8*

> *"12 Sow to yourselves in righteousness, reap in mercy; break up your fallow ground: for it is time to seek the LORD, till he come and rain righteousness upon you." Hosea 10:12*

We know that the thief will come to steal, to kill, and to destroy. But you must
> *" ... resist stedfast in the faith, knowing that the same afflictions are accomplished in your brethren that are in the world." 1st Peter 5:9*

We must always watch, for man has no knowledge of the time that his enemy may strike. Like fishes taken in an evil net or birds taken by deceit, so the sons of men are taken in an evil time when it comes suddenly on them. Although he strikes suddenly, let us not allow him the upper hand to breakup or penetrate the things over which God has put us.

This thief comes to steal as well. He comes to take what

does not belong to him and to do so without our consent. The Lord speaks to us in the bible saying:

> *"19 ¶ Lay not up for yourselves treasures upon earth, where moth and rust doth corrupt, and where thieves break through and steal:*
>
> *20 But lay up for yourselves treasures in heaven, where neither moth nor rust doth corrupt, and where thieves do not break through nor steal:" Matthew 6:19,20*

We must guard the treasures in our life, because they are the provision that God has given us. We must lift our families, friends and purpose continually in prayer before God. We must be mindful of our speech and conduct, and above all strive to glorify God in everything that we do. When we do these things, we close all the gates or entrances that the enemy uses to access our inheritance in Christ.

This thief intends to commit more than theft. He also comes to kill our dreams and ultimately us. His desire is to put an end to our access and right standing with GOD. He knows that if he does that, he will put an end to the peace of God in our life. Consequently, our joy will be gone resulting in a systematic cessation of our fruitfulness in the Spirit.

Today we live among many with regrets. These could be regrets from lost opportunity, divorce, poor judgment, or just simply being at the wrong place at the wrong time. Either way, it is still the same enemy at work to stop us from pressing toward our purpose, conquering our fears and living a victorious Christian life. Press on soldier, for the same spirit that raised our Lord from the dead now lives in you. He is able to keep you from falling. He will also keep you in perfect peace as He does everyone whose trust is in Him, and who focus his or her thoughts on Him. Press on therefore soldier for the mark of your destiny, which Christ has ordained for you.

Finally, he comes to destroy. He would like to ensure the theft, killing, or destruction of every target. When destroyed, a target becomes useless or ineffective. Today our society suffers in a state of moral decadence as pornography, homosexuality and other forms of sexual deviances and vulgarities are on the rise. We are also witnessing the destruction of the desire for holy living, purity of mind and of the spirit, and a passionate desire for the manifestation of the power of God in this generation. The family and the structure thereof is in the state of ruin while such new phrases as "dysfunctional family" and "single parent family" have become normal part of our vernacular. My brethren, this is the devil at work, to tear down, break up or demolish our sense of values and the character of our society.

> *"And this is the condemnation, that light is come into the world, and men loved darkness rather than light, because their deeds were evil." John 3:19*

Yes, the devil comes to destroy and indeed may have destroyed some attributes or fabrics of our lives and of our society, but thus says the Lord:

> *"Blow ye the trumpet in Zion, and sound an alarm in my holy mountain: let all the inhabitants of the land tremble: for the day of the LORD cometh, for it is nigh at hand;"*
> *Joel 2:1*

> *"And it shall come to pass, that whosoever shall call on the name of the LORD shall be delivered: for in mount Zion and in Jerusalem shall be deliverance, as the LORD hath said, and in the remnant whom the LORD shall call"*
> *Joel 2:32*

The Enemy of The Saints

We are the called. As the Lord has said:

"No man can come to me, except the Father which hath sent me draw him: and I will raise him up at the last day."

John 6:44

These are the last days. The love of many is waxing cold. We read and hear about so many things that make our ears tinkle, and with repeated bombardment of these senses, we find ourselves become more accepting of the very things we could not stand. There is slumber even in the camp, but awake from your slumber and stand as one of the remnants. Your God has given you all things that pertain to holiness along with the power to destroy the works of the devil. Remember, that God is your sure foundation and will not forsake you when persecution comes. Although, you may be for the moment cast down, the devil cannot destroy you.

THE NAMES OF YOUR ENEMY

Satan

In the Hebrew language, the word Satan means an adversary or one who withstands. Therefore, without any further delay let me introduce you to your enemy and adversary, Satan. Your enemy is not your spouse, biological family, or church family, not your friends or even your boss who you would love to hate. You have an adversary who as a roaring lion, walks about, seeking whom he may devour. He roams about constantly and is not afraid to go even into the house of God. We find that the more we desire to present ourselves before the LORD, with a desire to know Him better and serve Him more earnestly, the more vigorously Satan tries to intimidate and perhaps devour us.

He uses this common pattern on every child of God. He did the same thing to Joshua the son of Josedech, who was the high priest during the time of Haggai the prophet. The LORD had stirred up his spirit, and that of Zerubbabel, governor of Judah, and all the remnant of the people to rebuild the LORD's house – the Temple. When these came and began their work on the house of the LORD Almighty, their God, we find Satan standing at the right hand of Joshua the high priest, to intimidate him. He was not there when they were not rebuilding the house of the Lord.

> *"1 And he shewed me Joshua the high priest standing before the angel of the LORD, and Satan standing at his right hand to resist him.*
> *2 And the LORD said unto Satan, The LORD rebuke thee, O Satan; even the LORD that hath chosen Jerusalem rebuke thee: is not this a brand plucked out of the fire?"*
>
> *Zechariah 3:1; 2*

However, when he answered his call and began to walk in his calling, functioning as a high priest in the house of the Lord, Satan tried to restrain him from performing his duty. The Bible tells us that we

> *"... are a chosen generation, a royal priesthood, an holy nation, a peculiar people; that ye should shew forth the praises of him who hath called you out of darkness into his marvellous light:" 1st Peter 2:9*

God has chosen us to serve as priests in a temple, not made by hand, which is our body. As you walk in this calling, offering sacrifices of praises and thanksgiving unto God, your adversary will come to withstand you. Our calling is not only to glorify God in our body but also to rescue a dying world.

> *'To open their eyes, and to turn them from darkness to light, and from the power of Satan unto God, that they may receive forgiveness of sins, and inheritance among them which are sanctified by faith that is in me.' Acts 26:18*

The Enemy of The Saints

This again my brethren, without any doubt provokes resistance from Satan. Howbeit this one thing is certain, and that is the ever-abiding presence of our advocate, even Christ Jesus, Our Lord and Savior. He stands ready always to defend us as He rebukes our enemy on our behalf. That is not all, for to us is given not only the power to resist Satan but also to destroy all his works.

> 'And the God of peace shall bruise Satan under your feet shortly. The grace of our Lord Jesus Christ be with you. Amen.' Romans 16:20

The Serpent

The Lord declared:

> "Verily, verily, I say unto you, He that entereth not by the door into the sheepfold, but climbeth up some other way, the same is a thief and a robber." John 10:1

This statement leads us to know that it is possible for the same person to be a thief and a robber. You see whereas when a robber comes to take our property, he attacks openly using or threatening the use violence or force. The thief on the other hand takes our property secretly avoiding detection by moving carefully. Satan, also called the serpent, uses the same crafty underhandedness that the thief uses, when he comes to beguile the children of God.

> 'Now the serpent was more subtil than any beast of the field which the LORD God had made. And he said unto the woman, Yea, hath God said, Ye shall not eat of every tree of the garden?' Genesis 3:1

Beneath that subtle display is a poisonous and malicious enemy lying concealed in hedges and in cracks in walls, waiting for a prey. My brethren, we have to be alert,

'... lest by any means, as the serpent beguiled Eve through his subtilty, so your minds should be corrupted from the simplicity that is in Christ.' 2nd Corinthians 11:3

He uses his cunningness to blind the minds and the spiritual eyes of the children of men. If we allow the serpent to blind our hearts and minds, we become disobedient unto God. Consequently, we enlarge the gaps in the walls of our defense and lower the hedge of God's protection in our lives. In that passage, Christ also teaches us that it is possible to enter into the sheepfold some other way. It is about this other way that Jude warns the Church:

3 ¶ Beloved, when I gave all diligence to write unto you of the common salvation, it was needful for me to write unto you, and exhort you that ye should earnestly contend for the faith which was once delivered unto the saints.

*4 **For there are certain men crept in unawares, who were before of old ordained to this condemnation,** ungodly men, turning the grace of our God into lasciviousness, and denying the only Lord God, and our Lord Jesus Christ.*

Jude 1:3,4

In other words, a thief has penetrated the body of Christ. But this thief did not come through the door, for Jesus said:

1 Verily, verily, I say unto you, He that entereth not by the door into the sheepfold, but climbeth up some other way, the same is a thief and a robber.

2 But he that entereth in by the door is the shepherd of the sheep.

7 Then said Jesus unto them again, Verily, verily, I say unto you, I am the door of the sheep.

8 All that ever came before me are thieves and robbers: but the sheep did not hear them.

9 I am the door: by me if any man enter in, he shall be

The Enemy of The Saints

saved, and shall go in and out, and find pasture.
John 10:1-2; 7-9

This thief comes to shake our faith, which is the very foundation of our hope. In addition, to disrupt the confidence that we have in God through Christ our Savoir, However, the Lord said:

*"32 But **I have prayed for thee, that thy faith fail not:** and when thou art converted, strengthen thy brethren."*
Luke 22: 32

God's intent for us is that we overcome every obstacle that the enemy may present. He expects us to come out of every test better groomed for ministry and better able to lead others to Him with great joy:

"6...though now for a season, if need be, ye are in heaviness through manifold temptations:

7 That the trial of your faith, being much more precious than of gold that perisheth, though it be tried with fire, might be found unto praise and honour and glory at the appearing of Jesus Christ:" 1Peter 1:6-7

For this reason, Paul cautions:

"Cast not away therefore your confidence, which hath great recompence of reward." Hebrew 10:35

"Neither let us tempt Christ, as some of them also tempted, and were destroyed of serpents." 1st Corinthians 10:9

God has given us the power to bring this serpent under subjection to the rule of God in our lives. Yes, he will come from time to time to bruise your heel but remember when this happens, that his head is right by your feet and you are required to crush it.

As you resist him, he will look for new ways to steal from you.

> *"And the serpent cast out of his mouth water as a flood after the woman, that he might cause her to be carried away of the flood." Revelation 12:15*

Do not be surprised when men shall revile you, and persecute you, and shall say all manner of evil against you falsely for Christ's sake, for it is only the serpent pouring water out of its mouth at you. Do not be afraid of the serpent rather reverence God, give honor and glory to Him and hold on to Him for your help is on the way:

> *"So shall they fear the name of the LORD from the west, and his glory from the rising of the sun. When the enemy shall come in like a flood, the Spirit of the LORD shall lift up a standard against him." Isaiah 59:19*

The Devil, the Accuser of Our Brethren

The name Devil simply means slanderer. A slanderer is by definition, one who defames or injures another by maliciously uttering a false report. As fitting his name, the devil seeks to expose the children of God to contempt and shame using false statements or misrepresentation.

> *'...for the accuser of our brethren is cast down, which accused them before our God day and night.'*
> *Revelation 12: 10b*

He is not afraid to charge the saints falsely or with malicious intent, neither is he afraid to try to tarnish or impair our good name and reputation, which Christ has given us. The point worth noting here is that the devil will tell a

> **If you do not tell your 'story' to God, your accuser will tell Him his version of your 'story'.**

The Enemy of The Saints

lie on God through false interpretation of the scriptures as he did with Eve. This he accomplishes either by speaking directly to us as he did with Christ after his fast in the wilderness or by using corrupt vessels who seek the praise of men more than the unction from God.

In addition, the devil seeks to lie to God about us by bringing up our past from which Christ has purchased and separated us unto himself. He also brings up to God, all the sins that we have not confessed. For this reason my brethren, let us not harbor any sin in our life but rather confess them to our God who is merciful, just and willing forgive them as He washes our unrighteous spots away. Let me remind you however, that if you do not tell God "your story", your accuser will tell Him his version of "your story".

This enemy will lie to you about me while at the same time lying to me about you. I remember many years ago, how the enemy attacked the daughter of one of my co-laborer in our prayer room ministry. This daughter was gravely sick, and everyone in the ministry had been praying for her. She seemed to be getting better as we prayed. One Sunday while we were ministering, for no apparent reason, my co-laborer got very angry and started accusing me of things that were unimaginable. These accusations brought confusion to the team and shocked everyone because ours was a group that genuinely cared for one another. The following Saturday, my wife and I went to the church to minister to an individual. While there, another minister came and informed us that the co-laborer's daughter was unresponsive and at the point of death. This minister also told us that the hospital invited my co-laborer to have her last visit with her daughter. We knew the daughter's first name but not the last name since it was different from her mother's last name.

Nevertheless, I was determined to visit her, and trusted God to lead me to her, and He did. When I got to the hospital, God's favor allowed me access to all patients with the same first name as the daughter. I went to several rooms and each time the Holy Spirit would say this is the not the person. When I got to her room, God revealed to me that she was the person I was looking for, but strangely, He said to me, "Do not touch her but pray silently for her from a distance". I did as God had commanded me, then went to the nurses' station and obtained the last name of the patient for whom I had just prayed. Later on, I called my co-laborer who confirmed her daughter's last name and told me that she was at the hospital with the physicians when I visited her daughter. To the glory of God, two days later, her daughter became responsive and came out of her coma. Today she has recovered fully.

The point of this story is that all the devil wanted was to have that daughter. He knew that he could do nothing to hurt her while the church was praying. Therefore, he lied to her mother about me in order to create discord in our prayer group knowing that a house that is divided against itself cannot stand. Please my brethren, be careful who you listen to. Be careful who you allow to speak into your spirit. Remember that our mind is a battleground so,

"Keep thy heart with all diligence; for out of it are the issues of life." Proverbs 4:23 KJV

Remain on guard at all times knowing we contend not against flesh and blood. For;

"No man can enter into a strong man's house, and spoil his goods, except he will first bind the strong man; and then he will spoil his house." Mark 3:27 KJV

And,

"When a strong man armed keepeth his palace, his goods

are in peace:" Luke 11:21 KJV

We did not let the devil win for we knew then even as we know now, that all he wants to do is to sow "tares" in the garden of the Lord. He sows division, strive, envy and such like which does not glorify God. You may ask 'why does he lie so much?' Well, because:

"....He was a murderer from the beginning, and abode not in the truth, because there is no truth in him. When he speaketh a lie, he speaketh of his own: for he is a liar, and the father of it." John 8:44

The Tempter

"And when the tempter came to him, he said, "If thou be the Son of God, command that these stones be made bread"." Matthew 4:3

Our enemy is also the tempter. He tempts us according to what he perceives our wants to be. In general, he uses the lust of the flesh, the lust of the eye and the pride of life. Therefore, the more you sow in the flesh the more he has to work with. His perception of Christ was probably that after forty day of fasting, He should be hungry and consequently do any thing for food. Christ did not yield to this temptation because He knew that all that He needed was in the word of God. That should also be our position.

Secondly, he tested Christ for pride as well as His wisdom, understanding and application of the word of God. He did this first by enticing Him to do something that was not relevant to God's will and purpose for Him. Many of the called today have become trapped in this snare having been side tracked from their purpose; they now seek popularity with men and having become lifted up with pride have fallen into condemnation, driven of the devil.

We must be careful to discern the voice to which we are listening. For just because we find ourselves in a high position, does not imply that God led us there. Sometimes, the devil will push us up to a "high position" just so he can cause us to fall to our destruction. Remember he also came to destroy.

> *"Wherefore let him that thinketh he standeth take heed lest he fall." 1st Corinthians 10:12*

Thirdly, the devil will tempt us with the cares and riches of this world as he also did with Christ. Today, there are families destroyed because of the pressures and cares of this life. In many societies, honor and integrity have given way to dishonesty and corruption as people strive to accumulate wealth. Therefore,

> *"12 Blessed (happy, to be envied) is the man who is patient under trial and stands up under temptation, for when he has stood the test and been approved, he will receive [the victor's] crown of life which God has promised to those who love Him.*
> *13 Let no one say when he is tempted, I am tempted from God; for God is incapable of being tempted by [what is] evil and He Himself tempts no one.*
> *14 But every person is tempted when he is drawn away, enticed and baited by his own evil desire (lust, passions)." James 1: 12-14 (AMP)*

This drive for wealth and prosperity has infiltrated the church. For although John lets us know:

> *"Beloved, I wish above all things that thou mayest prosper and be in health, even as thy soul prospereth."*
> *3John 1:2*

He does not mean we should make that the object of our pursuit. However, some now distort God's set of guidelines for prosperity because they failed to test the spirits to ensure that they are in the will of God. Paul being worried about the work of the tempter in the church wrote:

"For this cause, when I could no longer forbear, I sent to know your faith, lest by some means the tempter have tempted you, and our labour be in vain."
1st *Thessalonians 3:5*

"No temptation has overtaken you except what is common to mankind. And God is faithful; he will not let you be tempted beyond what you can bear. But when you are tempted, he will also provide a way out so that you can endure it." 1st Corinthians 10:13(NIV)

OTHER NAMES AND TITLES OF YOUR ENEMY

Beside these principal names of our adversary, he also goes by other names and titles used to describe his actions and activities. Listed below are some of them.

- **Abaddon The angel of the bottomless pit**

  "And they had a king over them, which is the angel of the bottomless pit, whose name in the Hebrew tongue is Abaddon, but in the Greek tongue hath his name Apollyon." Revelation 9:11 (Apollyon in Greek means Destroyer)

- **Beelzebub, Prince of Devils**

  "But when the Pharisees heard it, they said, This fellow doth not cast out devils, but by Beelzebub the prince of the devils." Matthew 12:24

- **Belial (worthless, a rebel, destruction)**

  "Now the sons of Eli were sons of Belial; they knew not the LORD." 1st Samuel 2:12

"And what concord hath Christ with Belial? or what part hath he that believeth with an infidel?" 2nd Corinthians 6:15

- **The Dragon (The deceiver)**

"And the great dragon was cast out, that old serpent, called the Devil, and Satan, which deceiveth the whole world: he was cast out into the earth, and his angels were cast out with him." Revelation 12:9

"And he laid hold on the dragon, that old serpent, which is the Devil, and Satan, and bound him a thousand years," Revelation 20:2

"For many deceivers are entered into the world, who confess not that Jesus Christ is come in the flesh. This is a deceiver and an antichrist." 2nd John 1:7

- **The Enemy**

"The enemy that sowed them is the devil; the harvest is the end of the world; and the reapers are the angels."
Matthew 13:39

- **The Father Of All Lies, A Liar and A Murderer**

"Ye are of your father the devil, and the lusts of your father ye will do. He was a murderer from the beginning, and abode not in the truth, because there is no truth in him. When he speaketh a lie, he speaketh of his own: for he is a liar, and the father of it." John 8:44

- **Gates of Hell (Hades)**

"And I say also unto thee, That thou art Peter, and upon this rock I will build my church; and the gates of hell shall not prevail against it." Matthew 16:18

- **The Power of Darkness**

"Who hath delivered us from the power of darkness, and

The Enemy of The Saints

hath translated us into the kingdom of his dear Son:"
Colosians1:13

- **The Prince of This World**

    "Now is the judgment of this world: now shall the prince of this world be cast out." John 12:31

    "Hereafter I will not talk much with you: for the prince of this world cometh, and hath nothing in me" John 14:30

    "Of judgment, because the prince of this world is judged." John 16:11

- **The prince of the power of the air, The spirit that works in all disobedient people**

    "Wherein in time past ye walked according to the course of this world, according to the prince of the power of the air, the spirit that now worketh in the children of disobedience:" Ephesians 2:2

- **The Ruler of the darkness of this world**

    "For we wrestle not against flesh and blood, but against principalities, against powers, against the rulers of the darkness of this world, against spiritual wickedness in high places." Ephesians 6:12

- **The god of this world**

    "In whom the god of this world hath blinded the minds of them which believe not, lest the light of the glorious gospel of Christ, who is the image of God, should shine unto them." 2nd Corinthians 4:4

- **Unclean spirit**

    "When the unclean spirit is gone out of a man, he walketh through dry places, seeking rest, and findeth none."
    Matthew 12:43

- **The wicked one**

    "When any one heareth the word of the kingdom, and understandeth it not, then cometh the wicked one, and catcheth away that which was sown in his heart. This is he which received seed by the way side." Matthew 13:19

    "The field is the world; the good seed are the children of the kingdom; but the tares are the children of the wicked one;" Matthew 13:38

Now we know his names and some of his traits. He may think highly of himself and may even believe that he can oppress you and perhaps suppress your purpose. However, if God be for us, who can be against us? Remember that through God, we can withstand our enemies; and through His Name, we can trample everything that rises up against us under our feet.

However, since Christ was tempted and suffered for us in the flesh, let us be prepared to "drink of the cup", which He also drank, "for the servant is not greater than the master".

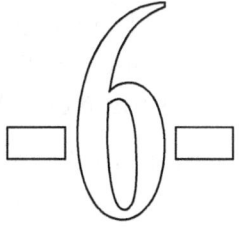

THE ORGANIZATION OF YOUR ENEMY

So far, I have discussed the names, objectives, and targets of our enemy. One thing is obvious. In order for this enemy to reach his targets of interest and accomplish its set objectives, it must itself be very organized. The bible tells us that:

'... we wrestle not against flesh and blood, but against principalities, against powers, against the rulers of the darkness of this world, against spiritual wickedness in high places' Ephesians 6:12

Right there we see a clearly stated chain of command and hierarchical organization. In the bible, we see that God assigns His angels to nations and kingdoms to guide their affairs as He interacts with their rulers. Consider for instance in the bible, for Egypt we read:

"15 And Pharaoh said unto Joseph, I have dreamed a dream, and there is none that can interpret it: and I have heard say of thee, that thou canst understand a dream to interpret it. Genesis 41:15

"25 And Joseph said unto Pharaoh, The dream of Pharaoh is one: God hath shewed Pharaoh what he is about to do." Genesis 41:25

It was God's presiding angel over Egypt who revealed to Pharaoh what God was about to do. A similar instance occurred in Babylon where King Nebuchadnezzar said:

> *"13 I saw in the visions of my head upon my bed, and, behold, a watcher and an holy one came down from heaven;" Daniel 4:13*

These watchers are the Angels assigned over the affairs of these people. Note that while the main focus of these watchers is to make known the will of God concerning these kingdoms, It is their ruler's responsibility to obey God or like Nebuchadnezzar, discover the hard way as he said:

> *"34 ¶ And at the end of the days I Nebuchadnezzar lifted up mine eyes unto heaven, and mine understanding returned unto me, and I blessed the most High, and I praised and honoured him that liveth for ever, whose dominion is an everlasting dominion, and his kingdom is from generation to generation:*
> *35 And all the inhabitants of the earth are reputed as nothing: and he doeth according to his will in the army of heaven, and among the inhabitants of the earth: and none can stay his hand, or say unto him, What doest thou?"*
> *Daniel 4:34-35*

Before I address the other aspects of this subject I need to bring to your attention that in each of these cases that we have looked at, God always had a "seer" among the people, one through whom he would reveal His mysteries. Daniel and Joseph represent two of such people. God had called and prepared them for moments like these. Today, many in the Church have chosen to ignore the office of the prophet and as a result, they continue to grope and perish in their ignorance. Do you know prophets? Let God use them in your midst; they are God's gifts to the Church as it is written:

The Organization of Your Enemy

11 And he gave some, apostles; and some, prophets; and some, evangelists; and some, pastors and teachers;
12 For the perfecting of the saints, for the work of the ministry, for the edifying of the body of Christ:
13 Till we all come in the unity of the faith, and of the knowledge of the Son of God, unto a perfect man, unto the measure of the stature of the fulness of Christ:
14 That we henceforth be no more children, tossed to and fro, and carried about with every wind of doctrine, by the sleight of men, and cunning craftiness, whereby they lie in wait to deceive;
15 But speaking the truth in love, may grow up into him in all things, which is the head, even Christ:
16 From whom the whole body fitly joined together and compacted by that which every joint supplieth, according to the effectual working in the measure of every part, maketh increase of the body unto the edifying of itself in love.
Ephesians 4:11-16

PRINCIPALITIES

Just as God has assigned his angels to preside over the affairs of nations, the devil has also done the same. Leading in this ranking of satanic forces is principality. Also called princedoms and princes, these spirit beings have the authority of a prince over nations, states, and even down to the households. These strongholds are responsible for controlling the affairs of the territory over which they have jurisdiction. The bible, tells us of the prince of Persia and the prince of Greece.

"12 Then said he unto me, Fear not, Daniel: for from the first day that thou didst set thine heart to understand, and to chasten thyself before thy God, thy words were heard, and I am come for thy words.

13 But the prince of the kingdom of Persia withstood me one and twenty days: but, lo, Michael, one of the chief princes, came to help me; and I remained there with the kings of Persia." Daniel 10:12-13

"20 Then said he, Knowest thou wherefore I come unto thee? and now will I return to fight with the prince of Persia: and when I am gone forth, lo, the prince of Grecia shall come." Daniel 10:20

If you read the preceding verses carefully, you would notice that these were not ceremonial princes, but rather the rulers of these kingdoms. Today the principality of corruption rule some countries while greed and self-indulgence rule others. Immorality and all manner of uncleanness to mention but a few also have their grip on many nations.

In the preceding passage, the work of these principalities was to keep the children of Israel in exile and bondage by manipulating the hearts and policies of the rulers of Persia. Therefore, we now realize that these principalities can obstruct the purpose and destiny of a people or a nation. What have you been asking of God? If your prayer has been according to His will, could a principality be the hindrance?

We must also notice that although, these principalities are generally out to oppose the affairs of a people or nation, they do sometimes oppose individuals. As you grow in Christ Jesus, fervent in spirit; serving the Lord; walking in the power of His might, and taking authority over the works of darkness, these principalities will come after you as though you were a nation. Understand that as you walk in the Spirit, so you shall have influence to change the affairs in this world as it is written:

"If my people, which are called by my name, shall humble themselves, and pray, and seek my face, and turn from

The Organization of Your Enemy

their wicked ways; then will I hear from heaven, and will forgive their sin, and will heal their land."

2nd Chronicles 7:14

This ability by the people of God to move the "Hand of God" is what brings them into direct confrontation with these principalities as though they were nations. We know the story of Daniel, how he chose to consecrate himself to God rather than eat the king's food in Babylon. How he found favor with God and with the Kings. Armed with favors, he began his prayer that would change the lives of his people.

"18 O my God, incline thine ear, and hear; open thine eyes, and behold our desolations, and the city which is called by thy name: for we do not present our supplications before thee for our righteousnesses, but for thy great mercies.

19 O Lord, hear; O Lord, forgive; O Lord, hearken and do; defer not, for thine own sake, O my God: for thy city and thy people are called by thy name." Daniel 9:18-19

We must understand that when we move our focus from our personal needs, and begin to focus on the greater purpose that God has for us, principalities will begin to oppose us. Notice here that Daniel's desire was to see the fulfillment of the word of God concerning Israel. Notice also that the prince of Persia, who is the principality over the country Persia, in which Daniel lived, hindered the answer to Daniel's prayer. It is obvious therefore, that if you can "move" the "Hand of God" you can also draw the attention of these principalities.

This was also the case with Jesus Our Lord. He came not for His own glory, but to do the will of the Father and be the light to the people who sat in darkness, and a way of escape to whosoever wills. Here, the devil himself opposed Him in the wilderness; but Christ was victorious over him. When was the last time you desired the good for others above your personal needs.

One interesting observation here is that as one principality is subdued, another would take its place, but *God is our refuge and strength, a very present help in trouble*. Therefore, do not be afraid of the 'prince of Persia' neither live in fear because of the 'prince of Greece'. Rather, focus on the race that is set before you and pursue your purpose steadfastly,

> *"Looking unto Jesus the author and finisher of our faith; who for the joy that was set before him endured the cross, despising the shame, and is set down at the right hand of the throne of God." Hebrews 12:2*

POWERS

Now, remember that we do also wrestle against powers. These are spiritual potentates, whose realm is among those in lead roles. We must understand that although most people regard power as a product of delegated authority, often times those who possess influence can exercise greater power than those with delegated authority in an arena in which they both exist. With this in mind therefore, we should know that no one is exempt from the opposition from this class wickedness. Although you may not hold any position with delegated authority, yet through relationships, you do influence someone's life. This life could be that of your parents, siblings, spouses, children, relatives, friends, colleagues, your fellow Christians and yes even those who follow you from afar off. The point here is that everyone will experience the activities of these powers.

The same argument is also true that the devil can use whosoever has authority or influence over you in an effort to hinder you. In the bible, we read that Jesus called Simon, Satan, shortly after he had changed his name to Peter. This

The Organization of Your Enemy

was because Satan had entered into Peter and through him, tried to influence Christ's obedience to God and in a yet larger sense, God's plan for our salvation. Notice that Jesus recognized him immediately and so should every child of God.

These powers were also at work in the minds of the presidents and princes of Persia over whom, the king had placed Daniel.

> *"1 ¶ It pleased Darius to set over the kingdom an hundred and twenty princes, which should be over the whole kingdom;*
> *2 And over these three presidents; of whom Daniel was first: that the princes might give accounts unto them, and the king should have no damage.*
> *3 Then this Daniel was preferred above the presidents and princes, because an excellent spirit was in him; and the king thought to set him over the whole realm.*
> *4 Then the presidents and princes sought to find occasion against Daniel concerning the kingdom; but they could find none occasion nor fault; forasmuch as he was faithful, neither was there any error or fault found in him."*
> *Daniel 6:1-4*

Driven by envy, jealousy and hatred, they sought ways to destroy Daniel. Here we see conspiracy in action as well as conniving schemes developed by the enemy for use in the execution of his plan. When powers are at work, they use those with influence and authority. The devil probably knew that as long as the excellent spirit was in Daniel, he would be nothing but trouble for him. Therefore, he attacked his prayer life. Can you see yourself in this picture? Is there an excellent spirit in you? Do you have a prayer life? Satan has no reason to try to destroy you if you are powerless and under his control, because he knows that one day, you will suffer with him forever. However, if you should choose to love the Lord thy God and to serve Him, then be assured that:

"....Thy God whom thou servest continually, he will deliver thee." Daniel 6:16

Powers operations are also active in the church. Some of the denominations that we have established, are neither according to divine order nor perfect will of God. For God's will and desire concerning His church is:

"21 That they all may be one; as thou, Father, art in me, and I in thee, that they also may be one in us: that the world may believe that thou hast sent me.
22 And the glory which thou gavest me I have given them; that they may be one, even as we are one:
23 I in them, and thou in me, that they may be made perfect in one; and that the world may know that thou hast sent me, and hast loved them, as thou hast loved me." John 17:21-23

Today we bite and devour one another, because of prevailing rebellious spirits. We produce bastard organizations not fully grounded in the doctrine of Our Lord Jesus Christ. In addition, because of strife, consume one another over the airwaves and from our pulpits. These things are not of God but an enemy has done these.

We have to watch to ensure that we abuse neither the authority delegated to us by God nor the influence that He has given us with men.

The Organization of Your Enemy

THE RULERS OF THE DARKNESS OF THIS WORLD

The bible tells us that we are not only fighting against *powers, but also against the rulers of the darkness of this world.* These world rulers of this present darkness are responsible for the promotion and perpetuation of ignorance with respect to the things and the will of God for man. They are also responsible for the spread and growth of all manners of ungodliness that we find in this world today. These world forces also called the prince of this age, have rule over the hearts and minds of those who would not fully embrace the grace of our Lord Jesus Christ. Of whom Paul writes:

"3 But if our gospel be hid, it is hid to them that are lost: 4 In whom the god of this world hath blinded the minds of them which believe not, lest the light of the glorious gospel of Christ, who is the image of God, should shine unto them." 2nd Corinthians 4:3-4

The principal weapons of these forces are spiritual blindness and ignorance. With these weapons, the enemy has caused many to walk in the vanity of their mind, and give themselves over unto lasciviousness, to work all uncleanness with greediness.

"18 Having the understanding darkened, being alienated from the life of God through the ignorance that is in them, because of the blindness of their heart:" Ephesians 4: 18

So today, we find natural and spiritual destruction looming in the air for many because of ignorance. Many people perish, dreams are lost, and hopes destroyed for lack of knowledge. They have become bound for hell, led by the rulers of this present darkness.

The unfortunate part of this is that these forces have found their way into the church, and have driven many to the state of compromise. They are at work constantly to sow strife and cause division in the body of Christ, tools they use often to drive many from the fold. Many have become lovers of themselves rather than lovers of God as they submit themselves to the rulers of this world system.

> *"10 His watchmen are blind: they are all ignorant, they are all dumb dogs, they cannot bark; sleeping, lying down, loving to slumber.*
> *11 Yea, they are greedy dogs which can never have enough, and they are shepherds that cannot understand: they all look to their own way, every one for his gain, from his quarter.*
> *12 Come ye, say they, I will fetch wine, and we will fill ourselves with strong drink; and to morrow shall be as this day, and much more abundant." Isaiah 56:10-12*

Here we see the neglect or abuse God's grace once influenced by this satanic force. Therefore, such can neither connect with God nor perceive Him and His purpose for their lives. When they should be calling on God for their salvation, they have become "full of themselves" driven by pride to their fall and by a haughty spirit to their destruction.

> *"21 Because that, when they knew God, they glorified him not as God, neither were thankful; but became vain in their imaginations, and their foolish heart was darkened.*
> *22 Professing themselves to be wise, they became fools,*
> *23 And changed the glory of the uncorruptible God into an image made like to corruptible man, and to birds, and fourfooted beasts, and creeping things.*
> *24 Wherefore God also gave them up to uncleanness through the lusts of their own hearts, to dishonour their own bodies between themselves:*
> *25 Who changed the truth of God into a lie, and worshipped and served the creature more than the Creator, who is*

The Organization of Your Enemy

blessed for ever. Amen.
26 For this cause God gave them up unto vile affections: for even their women did change the natural use into that which is against nature:
27 And likewise also the men, leaving the natural use of the woman, burned in their lust one toward another; men with men working that which is unseemly, and receiving in themselves that recompence of their error which was meet.
28 And even as they did not like to retain God in their knowledge, God gave them over to a reprobate mind, to do those things which are not convenient;
29 Being filled with all unrighteousness, fornication, wickedness, covetousness,
maliciousness; full of envy, murder, debate, deceit, malignity; whisperers,
30 Backbiters, haters of God, despiteful, proud, boasters, inventors of evil things, disobedient to parents,
31 Without understanding, covenantbreakers, without natural affection, implacable, unmerciful:
32 Who knowing the judgment of God, that they which commit such things are worthy of death, not only do the same, but have pleasure in them that do them."
Romans 1:21-32

What more is there to say? But that it is a sad state to be without God and His Spirit which raises a standard for you against the enemy of your soul. We need to be on guard as we watch for signs of compromise, which are the works of the ruler of this world. In addition, we must fight him even when he comes as an angel of light by resisting him and all his wiles. We must be instant in season, and out of season, never compromising, holding unto the truth and light of our Lord Jesus Christ. For,

> *"5 Ye are all the children of light, and the children of the day: we are not of the night, nor of darkness.*
> *6 Therefore let us not sleep, as do others; but let us watch and be sober.*
> *7 For they that sleep sleep in the night; and they that be drunken are drunken in the night.*
> *8 But let us, who are of the day, be sober, putting on the breastplate of faith and love; and for an helmet, the hope of salvation.*
> *9 For God hath not appointed us to wrath, but to obtain salvation by our Lord Jesus Christ,"*
> 1st Thessalonians 5:5-9

My brethren, since our God has delivered us from the power of darkness, and translated us into the kingdom of His dear son, let us therefore:

> *"6 Be anxious for nothing, but in everything by prayer and supplication, with thanksgiving, let your requests be made known to God;*
> *7 and the peace of God, which surpasses all understanding, will guard your hearts and minds through Christ Jesus." Philippians 4:6-7 (NKJV)*

The Organization of Your Enemy

SPIRITUAL HOSTS OF WICKEDNESS IN THE HEAVENLY PLACES

Just as powers and principality, work closely, so do the rulers of the darkness of this world and the spiritual hosts of wickedness in the heavenly places. These hosts of wickedness operate primarily in the air around us. Their work, is to afflict, oppress, destroy, attack, do battle, work destruction in the earth, and cause trouble for those who live in it. These spirits fight against the children of men by influencing them. They plant seeds of wickedness in their hearts as with Judas Iscariot, causing him to betray his own master.

"And supper being ended, the devil having now put into the heart of Judas Iscariot, Simon's son, to betray him;"
John 13:2

These evil spirits also known as demons, have always been at work putting evil thoughts in our minds.

"And GOD saw that the wickedness of man was great in the earth, and that every imagination of the thoughts of his heart was only evil continually." Genesis 6:5

The incident recorded in the bible of the encounter of Greek, Syrophenician woman and Our Lord Jesus Christ tells us that these evil spirits afflict people by sometimes taking up residence within them.

"25 For a certain woman, whose young daughter had an unclean spirit, heard of him, and came and fell at his feet: 26 The woman was a Greek, a Syrophenician by nation; and she besought him that he would cast forth the devil out of her daughter.
27 But Jesus said unto her, Let the children first be filled: for it is not meet to take the children's bread, and to cast it unto the dogs.

Fighting To Win - Volume One

28 And she answered and said unto him, Yes, Lord: yet the dogs under the table eat of the children's crumbs.

29 And he said unto her, For this saying go thy way; the devil is gone out of thy daughter.

30 And when she was come to her house, she found the devil gone out, and her daughter laid upon the bed."

Mark 7:25-30

When these evil spirits possess people, they cause them to become mentally unstable and oftentimes suicidal. They have power to cause seizure, to make their victim dumb, and to drive them to self-destruction.

"17 And one of the multitude answered and said, Master, I have brought unto thee my son, which hath a dumb spirit;
18 And wheresoever he taketh him, he teareth him: and he foameth, and gnasheth with his teeth, and pineth away: and I spake to thy disciples that they should cast him out; and they could not.
19 He answereth him, and saith, O faithless generation, how long shall I be with you? how long shall I suffer you? bring him unto me.
20 And they brought him unto him: and when he saw him, straightway the spirit tare him; and he fell on the ground, and wallowed foaming.
21 And he asked his father, How long is it ago since this came unto him? And he said, Of a child.
22 And ofttimes it hath cast him into the fire, and into the waters, to destroy him: but if thou canst do any thing, have compassion on us, and help us." Mark 9:17-22

These demons do not particularly care about how often we go to church, dance down the isles, or even quote the Scriptures. All they want to do is corrupt our minds in order

The Organization of Your Enemy

to make it impossible for us to receive from God, what our soul really desires. And oh! How well they have done their job. For Jesus himself said,

> *"This people draweth nigh unto me with their mouth, and honoureth me with their lips; but their heart is far from me."*
> *Matthew 15:8*

These wicked spirits pose great danger to the believers because they are unseen enemies, who creep discretely into the church to attack us and hinder our pursuit of excellence in Christ. They are the tares planted by the devil, to entice the saints, and provoke them to commit acts of disobedience such as adultery, fornication, uncleanness, lasciviousness, idolatry, witchcraft, hatred, variance, emulations, wrath, strife, seditions, heresies, envying, murders, drunkenness, reveling, and such like:

> *"2 Wherein in time past ye walked according to the course of this world, according to the prince of the power of the air, the spirit that now worketh in the children of disobedience:*
> *3 Among whom also we all had our conversation in times past in the lusts of our flesh, fulfilling the desires of the flesh and of the mind; and were by nature the children of wrath, even as others." Ephesians 2:2-3*

Yes in times past, we were spiritually blind and unable to discern spiritual things including the activities of these wicked spirits. However, because we now believe in our Lord Jesus Christ, God has blessed us with all spiritual blessings in heavenly places in Christ. We now have the indwelling presence of the Spirit of God, which causes us to walk in His statutes, and obey his commandments not by force, but by willingly submitting, because we now have the mind of Christ. If you believe in the finished work of Jesus Christ, I say this to you then arise! Resist the devil, be an example of the believer, in word, in conduct, in love, in spirit, in faith, in purity, and bear fruit worthy of your calling. If you set your focus on the Lord, to follow Him, you will be victorious over these evil spiritual forces in the heavenly realm. Remember that the Lord will keep those who trust in Him in perfect peace.

THE WEAPONS AND TRICKS OF YOUR ENEMY

Earlier we established that Satan goes back and forth in search of victims. He does so with well thought through objectives. He has an organization that is willing to do his dirty works. The believer's duty as a Christian soldier is to destroy these works of the devil. God has sent us forth as sheep in the midst of wolves. However, we go in His NAME, armed with His WORD, to fight the fight of faith, duly cautioned to be as wise as serpents, and as harmless as doves. This wisdom calls for the recognition and understanding of the weapons of our adversary. For our Lord said:

> *"31 Or what king, going to make war against another king, sitteth not down first, and consulteth whether he be able with ten thousand to meet him that cometh against him with twenty thousand?*
> *32 Or else, while the other is yet a great way off, he sendeth an ambassage, and desireth conditions of peace."*
> Luke 14:31-32 (KJV)

Our plan and strategy for engaging our enemy depends on which member of his organization we are facing, and the type of weapons they have. Therefore, we have to study the word of God for in it God has hidden the weapons that we need to overcome our enemy. Note, that Christ himself used the word of God to fight his way out of Satan's trap. When He says we should be as innocent as the doves, He is asking that we do not allow Satan to make us partakers of his corrupt ways or entangle us in his web of tricks, or lure us to disobey God as he did when he beguiled Eve through his subtleness.

For once Satan traps a victim in his web, he systematically begins to inflict that victim with his venoms, a process that will ultimately lead to death, if not stopped. You see the devil likes to hear our sad songs as much as he likes to be the master of ceremony at our "pity parties." However, we must fight back with the word of God. When we use the Word in battle, we must apply it properly and accurately. For instance, when the enemy sends the spirit of heaviness, sadness, and depression our way, we must counter that with the word and promises of God that guarantees joy and peace of mind. God's desire is that we remain victorious over every trick that the enemy may bring. For this reason, it is necessary to take a few moments to discuss some of the primary wiles of our common adversary so that we can adequately prepare to overcome them.

INTIMIDATION

The fact that the bible compares Satan's movement to that of a roaring lion, signals the presence of intimidation and fear. It is of this intimidation that Jesus spoke, when he warned his disciples saying:

> *"17 But beware of men: for they will deliver you up to the councils, and they will scourge you in their synagogues;*
> *18 And ye shall be brought before governors and kings for*

The Weapons and Tricks of Your Enemy

my sake, for a testimony against them and the Gentiles."
Matthew 10:17

It was not long after his ascension that the rulers of the temple threatened Peter and John after God had healed the man at the beautiful gate.

"17 But that it spread no further among the people, let us straitly threaten them, that they speak henceforth to no man in this name.
18 And they [the priests, and the captain of the temple, and the Sadducees] called them, and commanded them not to speak at all nor teach in the name of Jesus.
19 But Peter and John answered and said unto them, Whether it be right in the sight of God to hearken unto you more than unto God, judge ye.
20 For we cannot but speak the things which we have seen and heard.
21 So when they had further threatened them, they let them go, finding nothing how they might punish them, because of the people: for all men glorified God for that which was done." Acts 3:17-21

Today, this intimidation tactic is in great use. For among other things prayer in our public schools is under attack. In some communities, it is against the law to preach against immorality and homosexuality. In other instances, for naming the name of the Lord, Christians are imprisoned and enslaved. At a more individual level, families, friends, co-workers, and yes, even local church assemblies to say the least have ostracized, rejected, and scorned many of us. However, my brethren:

"Be not afraid of sudden fear, neither of the desolation of the wicked, when it cometh." Proverbs 3:25

Though you may feel hedged by these forces of intimidation, do not be afraid for your victory is on its way, besides, we know it can only last for a season. Whatever you do, do not quit. Keep the faith to the end.

"For I reckon that the sufferings of this present time are not worthy to be compared with the glory which shall be revealed in us." Romans 8:18

FEAR

The whole reason for the intimidation is to create fear. Many of us have fallen prey to this trick in one way or the other. Today in our society, we have given names to all kinds of fear, from the fear of the dark and of tight spaces to heights and just about anything, you can think of. This is not of God.

"For God hath not given us the spirit of fear; but of power, and of love, and of a sound mind." 2nd Timothy 1:7

There are yet other more subtle forms of fear that some have come to accept as a part of their character. They simply say, "This is who I am, or it's just how I am." Either way, it is still the trick of the enemy. Among these kinds of fear is the fear of intimacy. Many of us find it very difficult to open up to others. This fear of intimacy affords the devil the tool he uses to destroy marriages and relationships. For in our attempt to cover our weaknesses, we often tend to breakdown the communication channels between us and the ones we love, and those with whom God would desire to link us.

> **At one point or another but certainly at some point in our life, we will come face to face with our fears. However, our faith in Christ Jesus our Lord can swallow up the fears and threats from the devil and his messengers.**

God does not intend that we live our lives in isolation. He created us to be a part of a society, joined to others, to supply the needs of others and in so doing allow our needs to be satisfied. Even from the cross, Jesus took time to connect His mother with John, the disciple whom He loved. I believe that in this generation, God is still linking our destinies with those of others. As He did with Peter and Cornelius, Ananias and Saul (who would later become Paul), Paul and Barnabas, Naomi and Ruth and the list go on. God sometimes require that we step out of our comfort zone and become vulnerable as it were, so He can have the glory in our lives. Think about the lives that we could lead to Christ if we would overcome the binding fear of intimacy. Where would the Gentiles be if Peter did not go to Cornelius' house? On the other hand, would Thomas have called Jesus "My Lord and my God" if he never saw His wounds? The point is that by overcoming the fear of intimacy, we can become better vessels and more suited for the master's use.

In many ways, fear is like a mirage. Some say that it is false evidence appearing real. Others define it as a sentiment that one feels because of their belief in the prospect of an imminent discomfort or threat. In either case, it toys with our hopes and exposes our weaknesses. Because of this, some have tried to ignore it; others have tried to deny it; and many more have tried to avoid it. However, we cannot hide from your fears forever. At one point or another but certainly at some point in our life, we will come face to face with our fears. Yes, someday, we will have to face our fears.

Remember that Moses had to go back to Egypt and face the Pharaoh. When his staff turned into a snake the magicians of Egypt followed suit. Some of our fears are not due to our imaginations. They are real. However, just as the snake from Moses' staff swallowed the snakes from the staffs of the Egyptians, so also can our faith in Christ Jesus our Lord swallow up the fears and threats from the devil and his messengers. For:

"The LORD is on my side; I will not fear: what can man do unto me?" Psalms 118:6

"13 I can do all things through Christ which strengtheneth me." Philemon 4:13

ACCUSATIONS

Still in his attempt to limit our resolve to do the will of God, Satan has caused many believers to be subjects of accusations and controversies. Those who step out of the society's norms, who grab unto the move of God, and who dare to be different for Christ's sake, for their faith, receive a bombard of accusations. Today, many ministers of the gospel who have chosen to trust God to confirm His word with signs and miracles; including healings, face constant accusation by some factions in the church that have chosen not to acknowledge the full potency of their God, as well as the society, acting out of their ignorance. Many in our generation are still wrestling with the apostolic and prophetic offices, and tend to accuse those in the body on whom these mantles rest.

However, accusation as the devil's tool is not reserved only for those in ministry. Any Christian who would dare to be different by boldly denouncing in character and practice, those things that are contrary to the teachings of the Gospel of Jesus Christ is subject to accusation at times in their walk. The bible tells us that there is an accuser of the brethren. His job is to watch and to accuse the believers day and night subjecting us to severe scrutiny in an attempt to hold us captive in our mind. This enemy is the devil, who sometimes attacks our conscience himself, or at other times would use those around us. Nevertheless, Peter admonishes us to have:

The Weapons and Tricks of Your Enemy

"... a good conscience, that when they defame you as evildoers, those who revile your good conduct in Christ may be ashamed." 1Peter 3:16 NKJV

TEMPTATION

In an earlier chapter, we identified Satan as the tempter, who not only tempted Christ but also tempts Christians at every level of spiritual maturity. To be tempted simply put, is to be enticed, lured, persuaded or induced by an event, thing or other sources of stimulus to which one would respond. Along this line of thoughts therefore, we can see why watching a single advertisement of an alcoholic beverage on television for instance, would have no effect on a person who has never tested any alcoholic beverage, but may drive even a casual drinker to look for one. On the other hand, a continual exposure to this advertisement may persuade even the non-drinker to try one.

In other words, we are likely to be lured and enticed by the things we desire or have a tendency to desire. In addition, it is possible to persuade or induce a person to rethink or even ignore their conviction if they are not deeply rooted in it. The bible tells us that the Spirit led Christ into the wilderness where He was tempted by the devil. While there, he fasted for forty days and at the end of which, was tempted in three areas.

First, by the things he desired, being food, for the bible tells us that, *"in those days he did eat nothing and when they were ended, he afterward hungered"*. The devil seized this desire for food and used as a bait to lure Christ into temptation.

*"3 **And** the devil said unto him, If thou be the Son of God, command this stone that it be made bread.*

4 And Jesus answered him, saying, It is written, That man shall not live by bread alone, but by every word of God."
Luke 4:3-4

Many of us have genuine needs. But, to what extent would we go to have our needs satisfied. What price are we willing to pay for our natural needs? Yes, Christ hungered but His desire for spiritual food superseded His need for natural food. Hence, He could resist the devil. I think there is a lesson in this for us.

Second, by the things he saw.

"5 And the devil, taking him up into an high mountain, shewed unto him all the kingdoms of the world in a moment of time.
*6 **And** the devil said unto him, All this power will I give thee, and the glory of them: for that is delivered unto me; and to whomsoever I will I give it.*
7 If thou therefore wilt worship me all shall be thine.
8 And Jesus answered and said unto him, Get thee behind me, Satan: for it is written, Thou shalt worship the Lord thy God, and him only shalt thou serve." Luke 4:5-8

Here the devil is trying to stir up greed and ambitious behavior in Christ, using the things that he showed to Him. Has he ever done this to you? Earlier in the book, I mentioned that he is after our soul. How much is our soul worth?

"36 For what shall it profit a man, if he shall gain the whole world, and lose his own soul?
37 Or what shall a man give in exchange for his soul?"
Mark 8:36-37

Third, he tested His desire to be submissive to the perfect will of the Father.

9 And he brought him to Jerusalem, and set him on a pinnacle of the temple, and said unto him, If thou be the Son

The Weapons and Tricks of Your Enemy

of God, cast thyself down from hence:
10 For it is written, He shall give his angels charge over thee, to keep thee:
11 And in their hands they shall bear thee up, lest at any time thou dash thy foot against a stone.
12 And Jesus answering said unto him, It is said, Thou shalt not tempt the Lord thy God.
13 And when the devil had ended all the temptation, he departed from him for a season." Luke 4:9-13

Jesus did not jump at the command of the devil and neither should you. There is a time and a place in our lives for every scripture but the unction of the Spirit of God should drive those moments and not the suggestions of the devil. For this reason, we must know the voice of our Father and submit to His will. We must also study to show or present ourselves approved unto God as those who would apply the scriptures properly and in its seasons. For, untaught and unstable people will twist the scriptures and continually misapply it to their own destruction. Today with this trick, Satan is destroying many ministries and believers, for being economically challenged; they propagate as well as succumb to false doctrines. Still, the bible records:

> **There is a time and a place in our lives for every scripture but the unction of the Spirit of God should drive those moments and not the suggestions of the devil.**

"13 Let no man say when he is tempted, I am tempted of God: for God cannot be tempted with evil, neither tempteth he any man:" James 1:13

God may test our resolve as he did with Abraham when He asked him to sacrifice Isaac. He may allow the devil to come after us as He did concerning His servant Job. However, be assured that:

> *"There hath no temptation taken you but such as is common to man: but God is faithful, who will not suffer you to be tempted above that ye are able; but will with the temptation also make a way to escape, that ye may be able to bear it." 1st Corinthians 10:13*

There is always a way of escape, which is Jesus Christ the Word of God, who is always with us. If you submit to His counsel, He will keep you in the hour of temptation, which shall come upon the entire world. Hence;

> *"Blessed is the man that endureth temptation: for when he is tried, he shall receive the crown of life, which the Lord hath promised to them that love him." James 1:12*

LUST

In a time of temptation, some are drawn and enticed into many foolish and hurtful lusts. I want to differentiate between a temptation, and lust. Temptation often evokes choice. It pitches our needs against our obedience to the will of God. It challenges our desire to do what we know to be right. On the other hand, some describe lust as "a passionate or overmastering desire or craving." This desire is not born out of need but rather out of greed, covetousness and concupiscence, which is a strong desire oftentimes, sensual in nature. Lust is a desire for what is forbidden, and craving for what cannot legally be attained.

Consider the case of David and Bathsheba,

> *"2 And it came to pass in an eveningtide, that David arose from off his bed, and walked upon the roof of the king's house: and from the roof he saw a woman washing herself; and the woman was very beautiful to look upon.*
> *3 And David sent and enquired after the woman. And one*

The Weapons and Tricks of Your Enemy

said, Is not this Bathsheba, the daughter of Eliam, the wife of Uriah the Hittite?
4 And David sent messengers, and took her; and she came in unto him, and he lay with her; for she was purified from her uncleanness: and she returned unto her house." 2nd Samuel 11:2-4

David lusted over her, committed adultery with her, and killed her husband. Then, the Lord sent His prophet Nathan to David to tell him:

"10 Now therefore the sword shall never depart from thine house; because thou hast despised me, and hast taken the wife of Uriah the Hittite to be thy wife.
11 Thus saith the LORD, Behold, I will raise up evil against thee out of thine own house, and I will take thy wives before thine eyes, and give them unto thy neighbour, and he shall lie with thy wives in the sight of this sun.
12 For thou didst it secretly: but I will do this thing before all Israel, and before the sun."
2nd Samuel 12:10-12

For:
"2 Ye lust, and have not: ye kill, and desire to have, and cannot obtain: ye fight and war, yet ye have not, because ye ask not.
3 Ye ask, and receive not, because ye ask amiss, that ye may consume it upon your lusts." James 4:2-3

So you see my brethren, that:
"14 ... every man is tempted, when he is drawn away of his own lust, and enticed.
15 Then when lust hath conceived, it bringeth forth sin: and sin, when it is finished, bringeth forth death."
James 1:14-15

God has promised to provide the need of all His children. However, He would only provide the desires of those whose ways are pleasing to Him, rather than that of those who desire to waste God's provision on lustful things. Lust is at the root of many sins. It is a "resident evil" embedded in our Adamic nature and used very often by the devil to revive our carnal tendencies. We must resist the devil and his lustful powers of persuasion. For it is written:

"15 Love not the world, neither the things that are in the world. If any man love the world, the love of the Father is not in him.

16 For all that is in the world, the lust of the flesh, and the lust of the eyes, and the pride of life, is not of the Father, but is of the world.

17 And the world passeth away, and the lust thereof: but he that doeth the will of God abideth for ever."

1st *John 2:15-17*

DECEPTION

Whereas temptation offers choices to us, from which we must decide which to choose or refuse to choose, deception conceals or camouflages the wrong choices and gives them air of acceptance. Do not wonder that the devil sometimes comes as an angel of light to mislead those who are not awake and watching. Obviously, deception is lies, but it is also fraud, some of which Satan devises carefully to suit our carnal tendencies. We have said time and again that the enemy is out seeking those whom he may devour. He desires to defraud or beguile us of the hope that we have in Christ as well as the guaranteed victory that awaits us, if we remain faithful to the end. The bible says that he uses cunning craftiness, which is false wisdom. This wisdom is of this world and not of Christ. For

"The heart is deceitful above all things, and desperately

The Weapons and Tricks of Your Enemy

wicked: who can know it?" Jeremiah 17:9

Out of it, come deceptions. People occasionally say; "my mind is playing games on me" but the truth is that it is not a game but a cleverly contrived trick designed to lead you down the wrong path. When this happens, notice here that no one else is involved. It is just you and you alone battling with your own mind as you try to sort things in your life. When we think about deceit, we often think of others as the source. That is not always the case, for we can deceive ourselves by nurturing and promoting the false wisdom in our heart and consequently, fall into the snares of our adversary.

Having said that, the devil does not always come to deceive or mislead us himself. He does use men, especially those whose opinions we are likely to accept without questioning.

"5 And Jesus answering them began to say, Take heed lest any man deceive you:
6 For many shall come in my name, saying, I am Christ; and shall deceive many." Mark 13:5-6

In these days, as many allow their desires, affections and yes, their greed to pull them in diverse directions, it is not difficult to find those who can fall prey to the deceit of these evil workers. These persons could be your friends, relatives, colleagues and the list goes on, who, in a moment of weakness or perhaps by virtue of their nature, become tools of the enemy. Yet continually, we hear the words of caution:

"Beware lest any man spoil you through philosophy and vain deceit, after the tradition of men, after the rudiments of the world, and not after Christ." Colossians 2:8

Beware lest you become a casualty of their deception. For these appeal to our natural senses and exploit our weaknesses in the things of the Spirit. They come with persuasive logics and trickery to sway us, using as an impetus, our trust. Therefore:

"Beloved, believe not every spirit, but try the spirits whether they are of God: because many false prophets are gone out into the world." 1st John 4:1

It is of absolute necessity, that the child of God be deeply rooted and grounded in the Scriptures since this is the only way that we can discern the deceptive wiles of the devil. For as said earlier, although Peter was very close to Jesus, and although he had just received a revelation from the Father, as to the identity of Christ, Jesus saw Satan's sudden entry of into him. Jesus also recognized Satan's plan to use Peter as a tool of persuasion and discouragement against Him. As children of God, we must not only know the will and purpose of God for us but must stand ready to defend it. We must also realize that everything that distracts us from our goal is a deceptive trick of the devil.

DECEITFUL WORKERS TEACHING STRANGE DOCTRINES

In the previous section, I wrote about the devil use of 'ordinary' people who, in a moment of weakness or perhaps by virtue of their nature, become tools the enemy uses for his deceptive activity. In this section, I submit to you that he also uses other cleverly devised schemes, which involves deceitful workers of the gospel.

We know that in the work environment, there are workers with varying skills and responsibilities, the same can be said of the church, which is the body of Christ. Additionally, as there are differing ethics and quality of work at the work environment, so it is also in the church. However, the bible says everyone should be careful how he or she builds upon the foundation of the church of which Christ himself is the chief corner stone.

The deceitful workers of iniquity as they are called,

The Weapons and Tricks of Your Enemy

promote different man made doctrines which they try to pass on as the truth. Watch out for them for:

"1 ¶ Now the Spirit speaketh expressly, that in the latter times some shall depart from the faith, giving heed to seducing spirits, and doctrines of devils;
2 Speaking lies in hypocrisy; having their conscience seared with a hot iron;" 1st Timothy 4:1-2

They spread the doctrines of the devil having themselves fallen prey to seducing spirits of the devil.

"For such are false apostles, deceitful workers, transforming themselves into the apostles of Christ."
2nd Corinthians 11:13

The point worth noting here is that these people are among us. Many respect some of them. We have heard in the past of the incident in Guyana where many died because they believed the teachings of a false teacher, who seduced them away from the truth of the gospel of Jesus Christ.

This however, is not an isolated case for in Nigeria, a certain man arose in the 1960s proclaiming himself as the Christ, also led many astray. These started as though they were apart of us but quickly began to show their true colors. The bible also records the existence of these false prophets and teachers who have sold out their calling to gain the world. For speaking of the children of Israel and the Church, the Apostle Peter wrote:

"1 ¶ But there were false prophets also among the people, even as there shall be false teachers among you, who privily shall bring in damnable heresies, even denying the Lord that bought them, and bring upon themselves swift destruction.
2 And many shall follow their pernicious ways; by reason of whom the way of truth shall be evil spoken of.

3 ¶ And through covetousness shall they with feigned words make merchandise of you: whose judgment now of a long time lingereth not, and their damnation slumbereth not." 2nd Peter 2:1-3

Watch out for these servants of corruption for God had revealed their works and tricks to Peter as he further describes them saying:

"18 For when they speak great swelling words of vanity, they allure through the lusts of the flesh, through much wantonness, those that were clean escaped from them who live in error.

19 While they promise them liberty, they themselves are the servants of corruption: for of whom a man is overcome, of the same is he brought in bondage."

2nd Peter 2:18-19

These messengers of the devil exploit the weaknesses and hopes of many believers. They creep in when we least expect, having disguised themselves as children of the light. They walk among us and learned our ways. They know our areas of vulnerability and struggles. Consequently, without fail, they attack us through those very avenues. Nonetheless, those who are rooted in Christ, who desire purity and a heart that is undefiled before God, will find a way of escape from these workers of iniquity. The only way to keep our hearts pure is to live our lives, unspotted by the world and its lustful tendencies, and our minds daily focused on a closer walk with God.

Deceitful workers of iniquity spread the doctrines of the devil having themselves fallen prey to seducing spirits of the devil.

We should come to that place in our walk, where we know the truth, for it is the truth, which gives us the freedom from these sorts. You see the more we become mature in the things of God, and get to know our place, purpose and destiny, the more difficult it becomes for us to be persuaded by these whose aim is to steal the confidence that we have in Christ as they attempt to rob us of the joy of our salvation.

DOUBT AND FAITHLESSNESS

"And immediately Jesus stretched forth his hand, and caught him, and said unto him, O thou of little faith, wherefore didst thou doubt?" Mathew 14:31

Another trick of the devil is to cast doubt on our ability to achieve the goals that God has set for us. To doubt simply means to waiver. It is not that you do not believe, just that you are having a second thought. Is that not what most of us do? Have a second thought as though the God who beckoned us to come is not able to keep us from falling. Doubt tends to taint our victory and ruin our testimony. It questions our implicit trust and reliance on God and His word and threatens our ability to claim the promises of God.

Oh, how Peter would have loved to tell the story of how he walked on water, but doubt tainted his testimony. Many of us started on the right path, but have since lost many opportunities for progress because of doubt. Indecisions caused by doubt have many businesses crippled. Ministries are stagnant because doubt would not let them 'go to the other side'. Need I say more? Well, Paul wrote:

"I will therefore that men pray every where, lifting up holy hands, without wrath and doubting." 1st Timothy 2:8

It is not enough to be blameless before God and man when it comes to having our prayers answered but as James has said,

"6 But let him ask in faith, nothing wavering. For he that wavereth is like a wave of the sea driven with the wind and tossed.

7 For let not that man think that he shall receive any thing of the Lord.
8 A double minded man is unstable in all his ways."
James 1:6-8

Steadfast reliance on God's will for us is the key that God uses to fulfill our desires. In the book of Revelations, God makes a particular point about His dislike of a wavering attitude. He said:

"15 I know thy works, that thou art neither cold nor hot: I would thou wert cold or hot.
16 So then because thou art lukewarm, and neither cold nor hot, I will spue thee out of my mouth."
Revelation 3:15-16

When people are not committed to a cause, oftentimes, they will manifest their lack of commitment in their lukewarm attitude toward that cause. A double-minded person is one who wavers; neither cold nor hot, he is unstable in all his ways, and therefore can receive nothing from God. But Jesus said:

"If ye abide in me, and my words abide in you, ye shall ask what ye will, and it shall be done unto you."
John 15:7

In other words, to get whatsoever you ask for, you must remain in Christ and continually be in fellowship with Him. We must faithfully wait on Him even during our difficult times, and like Him, endure our hardship as good soldiers of the cross. To be in fellowship with Him, His Word must dwell richly in you knowing that this WORD is Christ in you the hope of glory. This hope is our joyful and confident expectation, built on the foundation that is set on Christ. It is also, what eliminates our wavering tendencies. For we have:

"... confident of this very thing, that he which hath begun a good work in you will perform it until the day of Jesus Christ:" Philippians 1:6

The Weapons and Tricks of Your Enemy

No wonder the devil likes to attack our faith. Is it not just like him to go after our seeds? In the parable of the sower Jesus pointed out that Satan has different avenues with which to destroy the confidence that you have in the Word of God, which is the foundation of your faith. First, he may come after you with blatant disbelief as in the case of Thomas, who doubted the resurrection of our Lord, and whom Christ, admonished saying 'be not faithless, but believing' and again 'blessed are they that have not seen, and yet have believed'.

Second, he may come though affliction or persecution aimed at testing or destroying your faith.

"Therefore, my beloved brethren, be ye stedfast, unmoveable, always abounding in the work of the Lord, forasmuch as ye know that your labour is not in vain in the Lord." 1st Corinthians 15:58

Third, he may try to use the cares of this world, or the deceitfulness of its riches, or even the lusts for the things that draw us, as a means to choke the word in us, and make it unfruitful. This was the case with Asaph the Psalmist when he wrote Psalms 73

"2 ...my feet were almost gone; my steps had well nigh slipped.
3 For I was envious at the foolish, when I saw the prosperity of the wicked.
4 For there are no bands in their death: but their strength is firm.
5 They are not in trouble as other men; neither are they plagued like other men.
6 Therefore pride compasseth them about as a chain; violence covereth them as a garment.
7 Their eyes stand out with fatness: they have more than heart could wish.
12 Behold, these are the ungodly, who prosper in the world; they increase in riches." Psalms 73:1-7;12

Moreover, as doubt begins to creep in, he writes:

"13 Verily I have cleansed my heart in vain, and washed my hands in innocency.
14 For all the day long have I been plagued, and chastened every morning." Psalms 73:13-14

However, when he came to himself he realized that this way that seems good to him at that time, actually led to destruction. Therefore he repenting of his doubts and faithlessness, and records these words for our admonition:

"23 Nevertheless I am continually with thee: thou hast holden me by my right hand.
24 Thou shalt guide me with thy counsel, and afterward receive me to glory.
28 But it is good for me to draw near to God: I have put my trust in the Lord GOD, that I may declare all thy works." Psalms 73:23-24; 28

God's desire is that such as hear the word, receive it, and bring forth fruit, for he said:

"Ye have not chosen me, but I have chosen you, and ordained you, that ye should go and bring forth fruit, and that your fruit should remain: that whatsoever ye shall ask of the Father in my name, he may give it you." John 15:16

I spent this time on the weapons and tricks of enemy of the saints so that we may know our enemy.

"Lest Satan should get an advantage of us: for we are not ignorant of his devices." 2nd Corinthians. 2:11

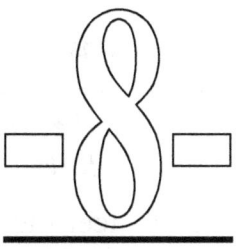

STAND IN THE EVIL DAY

In this volume, I have tried to let out the battle cry to the people of God. My hope is to alert us that we are walking through spiritual battlefields. I wanted also to expose the enemy of the saints and his the subtle ways. Therefore, time was spent discussing the nature and scope of spiritual warfare, with an intent however to point the child of God to a way of escape. God's desire is for the people who walk in darkness to see His great light. Hence, He lights up our pathway and guides our feet into the way of peace as He uncovers the works and traps that Satan has set for us. Knowing this to be true, we like King David can say:

"Yea, though I walk through the valley of the shadow of death, I will fear no evil; For You are with me; Your rod and Your staff, they comfort me." Psalms 23:4 NKJV

Yes, they do, and that is the point of our discussion here. You see, because the LORD our God goes with us to battles, to fight for us against our enemies, and to save us, we must remove all the accursed things from our "camp". For He said,

> *"18 And you, by all means abstain from the accursed things, lest you become accursed when you take of the accursed things, and make the camp of Israel a curse, and trouble it." Joshua 6: 18 NKJV*

It is one thing for us to feel the gentle staff of God that leads us to the way that we should go, but it is a terrible thing to feel the rod of the Almighty. As with the children of Israel, our God is the guarantor of our victory when we face our enemies, however, He requires us to obey His commandments. Remember "to obey is better than sacrifice."

The bible tells us what can happen to us when we violate our covenant with God by deliberately becoming tangled in sin.

> *"10 And the LORD said unto Joshua, Get thee up; wherefore liest thou thus upon thy face?*
> *11 Israel hath sinned, and they have also transgressed my covenant which I commanded them: for they have even taken of the accursed thing, and have also stolen, and dissembled also, and they have put it even among their own stuff.*
> *12 Therefore the children of Israel could not stand before their enemies, but turned their backs before their enemies, because they were accursed: neither will I be with you any more, except ye destroy the accursed from among you.*
> *Joshua 7: 10 – 12*

Understand my brethren that the scripture that we have just read is addressing a situation that occurred just after the fall of Jericho's wall. The children of Israel had just witnessed an awesome display of God's power. Rehab had just told them that the people of the land were afraid of them.

> *"9And she said unto the men, I know that the LORD hath given you the land, and that your terror is fallen upon us,*

and that all the inhabitants of the land faint because of you.
10 For we have heard how the LORD dried up the water of the Red sea for you, when ye came out of Egypt; and what ye did unto the two kings of the Amorites, that were on the other side Jordan, Sihon and Og, whom ye utterly destroyed.
11 And as soon as we had heard these things, our hearts did melt, neither did there remain any more courage in any man, because of you: for the LORD your God, he is God in heaven above, and in earth beneath." Joshua 2: 9 – 11

It was God's pleasure to give Israel the land, which He had promised. However, He did not change the conditions for possessing and occupying the land. For He had said to Abraham, walk before me and be thou perfect. This perfection has a two-fold implication.

First, God requires His people to be Holy as He is Holy.

"26 A new heart also will I give you, and a new spirit will I put within you: and I will take away the stony heart out of your flesh, and I will give you an heart of flesh.
27 And I will put my spirit within you, and cause you to walk in my statutes, and ye shall keep my judgments, and do [them]." Ezekiel 36:26-27

For this reason, He gave us a clean heart when we first believed in his Name. Additionally, He put His Spirit in us to notch us along the right path. However, this is a covenant relationship. For whereas the role of the Spirit is to show us the way, ours is to follow Him, walking by faith. God will points out the accursed things along the way, from which, we are to abstain. He always keeps His end of the covenant; we should likewise uphold our end.

Second, He desires that we grow up into him in all things, which is the head, even Christ. In the natural sense, when one grows up, they no longer fit their childhood clothes, so it should be with the child of God. For Paul said:

> *"When I was a child, I spake as a child, I understood as a child, I thought as a child: but when I became a man, I put away childish things."* 1st *Corinthians 13:11*

Because he continues,

> *"1 Now I say, That the heir, as long as he is a child, differeth nothing from a servant, though he be lord of all;*
> *2 But is under tutors and governors until the time appointed of the father.*
> *3 Even so we, when we were children, were in bondage under the elements of the world:" Galatians 4:1-3*

God said, "Be thou perfect." In other words, except we mature in Him, we will not be able to exercise all the rights and privileges that we have in God. We will not be able to bring to subjection, every thought to the obedience of Christ, but would remain in bondage under the elements and rulers of this present darkness. This was the case with the children of Israel. They had reached the promise land but they had not become mature enough to be trusted with a covenant. They were still fascinated by accursed things, as are some of us.

They were still taking the abiding presence of God for granted, presuming that God's presence would remain with them even with the accursed thing in the camp, as some of us also do. Although we know that it is in God that we live, move, and have our being and that without Him we are nothing, we still have tendencies to disobey Him. As most good parents would, God would not allow us to dishonor Him. His judgment summons Him to leave us, but His mercy begs for a show of grace. Then through His grace, He points us to the way of escape as His love cries out to us saying,

> *"11 Israel hath sinned, and they have also transgressed my*

Stand in The Evil Day

covenant which I commanded them: for they have even taken of the accursed thing, and have also stolen, and dissembled also, and they have put it even among their own stuff.
12 Therefore the children of Israel could not stand before their enemies, but turned their backs before their enemies, because they were accursed: neither will I be with you any more, except ye destroy the accursed from among you.
13 Up, sanctify the people, and say, Sanctify yourselves against to morrow: for thus saith the LORD God of Israel, There is an accursed thing in the midst of thee, O Israel: thou canst not stand before thine enemies, until ye take away the accursed thing from among you. Joshua 7:10 – 13

God will answer our prayers and deliver us from our adversaries, if we turn to Him with all our heart. Arise therefore from your ashes oh sleeping giant, and wash your feet in Emmanuel's blood. Let His Word sanctify you as He prepares you for the battles ahead. Remember that our work and battles continue until we see His face in glory. For when the prince of Persia is defeated, the prince of Greece will come and we cannot stand against them without the Anointed One and His Anointing. So keep your heart from evil thoughts and your mind set on Him and He will keep you in His perfect peace. If you humble yourself before the Lord and walk in obedience to His will, He declares:

> **God will answer our prayer and deliver us from our adversaries if we turn to him with our whole heart.**

"Ye shall not need to fight in this battle: set yourselves, stand ye still, and see the salvation of the LORD with you, O Judah and Jerusalem: fear not, nor be dismayed; to

morrow go out against them: for the LORD will be with you." 2ⁿᵈ Chronicles 20:17

In Volume two, we will take another look at Jesus Christ the author and the finisher of our faith, in whom dwells the fullness of the Godhead bodily and in whom, we are also complete. We will learn to know Him and by the time we are done, like Paul, we will find ourselves wanting the more to really know Christ and experience the mighty power that raised him from the dead. We will want to learn what it means to suffer with him, as Paul has said:

"That I may know him, and the power of his resurrection, and the fellowship of his sufferings, being made conformable unto his death;" Philippians 3:10

Remember He is not only the source of our faith, but He is also the object of our faith as it is written:

"28 And we know that all things work together for good to them that love God, to them who are the called according to his purpose.
29 For whom he did foreknow, he also did predestinate to be conformed to the image of his Son, that he might be the firstborn among many brethren.
30 Moreover whom he did predestinate, them he also called: and whom he called, them he also justified: and whom he justified, them he also glorified."
Romans 8:28-30

"Let the redeemed of the LORD say so, whom he hath redeemed from the hand of the enemy;" Psalms 107:2

When God redeemed us by His grace, He also gave us authority. I can imagine Him saying to Satan, "Satan I created you but because of your disobedience and pride I had Michael throw you out of heaven once. I am not going to belittle myself by coming after you. I am also not going to have

Stand in The Evil Day

Michael waste his time punching on you. Therefore I am going to create Man and I will make him a little lower than the angels, but I will give unto him power to bruise your head". By this time, you are probably thinking "but the bible was speaking of Christ" and you are right but remember:

> *"29 For whom he did foreknow, he also did predestinate to be conformed to the image of his Son, that he might be the firstborn among many brethren." Romans 8:29*

Moreover, Jesus said

> *"15 All things that the Father hath are mine: therefore said I, that he shall take of mine, and shall shew it unto you. John 16:15*

He also said,

> *"20 Neither pray I for these alone, but for them also which shall believe on me through their word;*
> *21 That they all may be one; as thou, Father, art in me, and I in thee, that they also may be one in us: that the world may believe that thou hast sent me.*
> *22 And the glory which thou gavest me I have given them; that they may be one, even as we are one:*
> *23 I in them, and thou in me, that they may be made perfect in one; and that the world may know that thou hast sent me, and hast loved them, as thou hast loved me."*
> *John 17:20-23*

> *Behold, I give unto you power to tread on serpents and scorpions, and over all the power of the enemy: and nothing shall by any means hurt you. Luke 10:19*

Yes, the power is ours through the Name of Jesus Christ. Additionally, just as God was with Israel all those years in the wilderness, nurturing, caring, guiding, delivering and preserving them, so is He also with us, His Spiritual Israel, who believe in Him through Christ Jesus our Lord. He continues to encourage us, saying:

> *"3 ... say unto them, Hear, O Israel, ye approach this day unto battle against your enemies: let not your hearts faint, fear not, and do not tremble, neither be ye terrified because of them;*
> *4 For the LORD your God is he that goeth with you, to fight for you against your enemies, to save you."*
> *Deuteronomy 20:3-4*

> *"Say to them that are of a fearful heart, Be strong, fear not: behold, your God will come with vengeance, even God with a recompence; he will come and save you."*
> *Isaiah 35:4*

> *"Be not afraid of the king of Babylon, of whom ye are afraid; be not afraid of him, saith the LORD: for I am with you to save you, and to deliver you from his hand."*
> *Jeremiah 42:11*

Fear cannot be a part of our armor when God is on our side. Therefore, we have to learn how to wear our God given armor and fight the good fight of faith. David taught us a good lesson during the time that he was preparing to fight against Goliath.

> *"33 And Saul said to David, Thou art not able to go against this Philistine to fight with him: for thou art but a youth, and he a man of war from his youth. 34 And David said unto Saul, Thy servant kept his father's sheep, and there came a lion, and a bear, and took a lamb out of the flock: 35 And I went out after him, and smote him, and delivered it out of his mouth: and when he arose against me, I caught him by his beard, and smote him, and slew him. 36 Thy servant slew both the lion and the bear: and this uncircumcised Philistine shall be as one of them, seeing he*

Stand in The Evil Day

hath defied the armies of the living God. 37 David said moreover, The LORD that delivered me out of the paw of the lion, and out of the paw of the bear, he will deliver me out of the hand of this Philistine. And Saul said unto David, Go, and the LORD be with thee. 38 And Saul armed David with his armour, and he put an helmet of brass upon his head; also he armed him with a coat of mail. 39 And David girded his sword upon his armour, and he assayed to go; for he had not proved it. **And David said unto Saul, I cannot go with these; for I have not proved them. And David put them off him. 40 And he took his staff in his hand, and chose him five smooth stones out of the brook, and put them in a shepherd's bag which he had, even in a scrip; and his sling was in his hand: and he drew near to the Philistine."** *1 Samuel 17:33-40*

Goliath the Philistine represents the giant that we face in our daily life. We also have some that come to discourage us as we prepare for battle. David understood that the battle was not about him, but rather about the glory of God. He knew that he could not win the battle because of his ability. Rather that his victory was in the Name of the God with whom he had a relationship and whose power to deliver was proven. David also knew that the armor of man would not bring victory so he

> **Rise from your ashes oh sleeping giant, and wash your feet in Emmanuel's blood. Let His Word sanctify you as He prepares you for the battles ahead.**
> **Remember that our work and battles continue until we see His face in glory. For when the prince of Persia is defeated, the prince of Greece will come. And we cannot stand against them without the Anointed One and His Anointing.**

relied instead on the armor of God. He had to overcome the fear of the external giant (Goliath) and the discouragement of an internal influences or fears (Saul). You have to know the armor that God has given you for your battle.

"Wherefore take unto you the whole armour of God, that ye may be able to withstand in the evil day," Ephesians 6:13a

David did not put on man's armor to go to war, and neither should we. He used the weapons that God had given him and so should we. He did not hide in the face of the enemy. Rather, once armed and released to fight, he went on the offensive. We must also go on the offensive as led by the Holy Spirit and take back by force, all that the devil had stolen from us. We are to set the oppressed at liberty, breakdown the walls of spiritual prisons for those who are bound, and proclaim liberty to all the captives.

We are to fight for the restoration of the Church to its position of power. Finally, we must demonstrate the gospel to the world through our words and actions and in so doing, cause those who sit in darkness to see the saving light of our Lord Jesus Christ.

".. and having done all, to stand.
14. Stand therefore, having your loins girt about with truth, and having on the breastplate of righteousness;
15. And your feet shod with the preparation of the gospel of peace;
16. Above all, taking the shield of faith, wherewith ye shall be able to quench all the fiery darts of the wicked.
17. And take the helmet of salvation, and the sword of the Spirit, which is the word of God:
18. Praying always with all prayer and supplication in the Spirit, and watching thereunto with all perseverance and supplication for all saints;" Ephesians 6:13b-18.

ABOUT THE AUTHOR

Onoyom E. Ekanem was born in Nigeria, West Africa. He received Christ as his personal savior at a young age and by revelation of God received the baptism of the Holy Spirit shortly thereafter. God called him to preach and teach the Gospel of JESUS CHRIST shortly after his new birth experience.

Pastor Ekanem began his ministry in the United States under the late Bishop David Lee Ellis, Pastor of Greater Grace Temple in Detroit, Michigan, and the Assistant Presiding Bishop of the Pentecostal Assemblies of the World. He continues to serve at Greater Grace Temple under the pastorate of Bishop Charles H. Ellis III, Presiding Bishop of the Pentecostal Assemblies of the World as the Assistant Pastor responsible for Evangelism and Outreach Ministries. Over the years, God has continued to use him to His glory. He is a prayer warrior and counselor with a mandate from God to free His people from the stronghold of Satan.

Rev. Ekanem is a Prophet of God, and a teacher of the Gospel. Over the past decades, he has taught numerous targeted courses aimed at helping the people of God to walk victoriously in their Christian life. These courses cover the areas of "Spiritual Maturity", "Spiritual Warfare and Deliverance", "The Authority of the Believer" and "Men on the Potter's Wheel", a targeted course for men. He also taught the "Ministerial Introduction Course" at a campus of Aenon Bible College housed in Greater Grace Temple.

Pastor Ekanem is a graduate of Aenon Bible College, and a licensed Minister of the Gospel under the umbrella of the Pentecostal Assemblies of the World, Inc. (PAW). He holds a Bachelor degree in Electrical/Electronic Engineering, from Lawrence Institute of Technology in Southfield Michigan, and a Master of Engineering Management Degree from the University of Detroit, Detroit Michigan.

Victorious Christian Life Series

CONTACT US

To contact Pastor Ekanem,

Send Email to:
vcl.publications@yahoo.com

You may also call us at (248) 796-7676

For additional copies of this book, please visit
http://www.createspace.com/3748598

Alternatively, write to
Victorious Christian Life Publications
376 Beach Farm Circle #367
Highland, MI 48357

Please contact us to request bulk quantity pricing.

Victorious Christian Life Series

www.ingramcontent.com/pod-product-compliance
Lightning Source LLC
Chambersburg PA
CBHW071505040426
42444CB00008B/1501